finding light in the darkness

a collection of blackout poetry

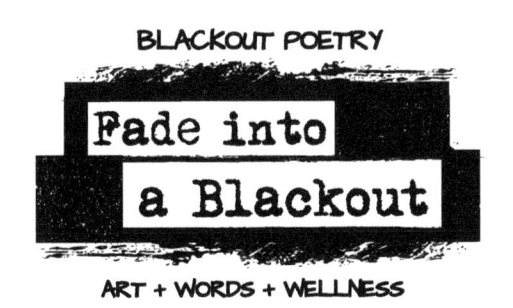

BLACKOUT POETRY
Fade into a Blackout
ART + WORDS + WELLNESS

Michael Nyers

Copyright © 2018 Michael Nyers

All rights reserved. This book or any portion thereof may not be reproduced or used in any manner whatsoever without the express written permission of the publisher except for the use of brief quotations in a book review.

First Printing, 2018

Dawn Valley Press P.O. Box 112 Beaver, PA 15009
DawnValleyPress.com

ISBN-13: 978-0-936014-24-1

Library of Congress Control Number: 2017958082

Cover design and layout: Michael Nyers

acknowledgements

This book is dedicated to my family and friends who have supported and encouraged me on this journey. I wouldn't be here without you. This is also going out to anyone out there suffering from any type of mental health illness or struggling with life in general. Remember: you are stronger than you know. Don't worry about what other people think. You're a badass! You got this!

I'm also thankful for old books, a good craft beer, laughing so hard you almost pee, and, of course, my dog Max, who is the only one who has stood beside me the entire time with loyalty and unconditional love.

A portion of the proceeds from this book will go to support various mental health organizations.

do not. stop press on

introduction

Creativity can be found just about anywhere in life. Art is life; life is art. But creativity is more than art. It's ubiquitous. It's using our imagination to solve problems.

Think of that chair you're sitting in right now or perhaps the electronic device you're reading this on. Did you ever stop to think that someone at some point had a vision and then used their creativity to turn that chair or computer screen into reality?

Creativity exists in each and every one of us. It's not a special talent gifted to certain people. We are all creative in our own way, and we have been since the day we were born. So what happened along the way to make us feel that we aren't creative? Think back to when you were a child. Perhaps you have a child of your own. Children are naturally creative. They can take a handful of crayons, a plain old cardboard box, and some household items and turn them into a half robot, half dinosaur thingamabob from outer space named Charlie. It's fascinating.

As we grow older, however, we become "educated" and taught to follow society's rules and regulations. We become stuck in our boxes of conformity, surrounded by barriers and walls of what the world tells us we should be. I'm not here to tell you that you can learn to be creative; I'm here to show you and remind you that it's been there all along.

OK, so now you're thinking, *"What the heck is this guy talking about, and what does it have to do with blackout poetry?"* That's a good question. The truth is I like to talk...a lot. Fun fact: when I am with a group of friends and the words "long story short" come out of my mouth, it's already too late. I'm a people person — Libra and ENFJ. (We'll just leave it at that.)

So, where were we again? Right! You. Creativity. Blackout poetry. Life. What does that mean to me? What *can* it mean for you? Let me tell you a little story (don't worry, I'll try to keep it short)...

About seven years ago I was leading the pretty standard life. I had a great career as an art director/graphic designer/web designer, a beautiful house and wife, and I was surrounded with plenty of friends, singing in a band on the side and just loving life. But life rarely goes as planned. I can't narrow it down to a particular moment, it just seemed that one day my stress and anxiety had started to rise. Overloaded at work, marital issues began to surface and other personal matters were starting to take their toll. Pretty soon, I was in the middle of a divorce, lost my dream house, and ended up at my dad's for a while because my other house (which wasn't selling) was being rented out (got screwed out of that), and a huge ripple effect began. I found myself in the middle of a deep depression, my anxiety was through the roof, and my OCD tendencies, which I felt worked to my advantage, spiraled out of control. I couldn't focus and concentrate at work and, as a result, was eventually let go. I was absolutely devastated.

After being on unemployment for about a month, I realized that I was in no shape to be working. I needed to sort things out. I applied for disability for mental health reasons and started going to counseling and a psychiatrist. I was diagnosed with Major Clinical Depression, severe Generalized Anxiety Disorder, and severe OCD. Suddenly I found myself at rock bottom. Family strife entered the mix. I lost some close friends and a girl who, despite being the best friend and relationship I ever had, decided to leave me. This wasn't just rock bottom. It was rock bottom's basement. I literally couldn't function. Suicide was seemingly a viable option to end the pain and suffering. And after a couple failed attempts, I was at the lowest point in my life. Even writing this right now is one of the hardest things I've ever done.

So, long story short (yeah, right)…enter blackout poetry!

One day as I was browsing the Web, I stumbled across an image of a blackout poem. I found it so fascinating that I immediately ran out and bought a book and a sharpie marker. I thought I would give it a try and hope that it would hold my attention for at least a couple of weeks. I did a few blackout poems and posted them on my personal Instagram account with the hashtag "#blackoutpoetry."

All of a sudden, I started getting some likes and comments on them. I thought to myself, *"Who the heck are these people?"* As it turns out, there is an entire community out there revolving around blackout poetry! Not only was this community kind and encouraging, but they also gave me the courage to start a separate account for my work. It was as if I finally had a breakthrough. The universe had intervened.

Over time I grew into the community, and the support and work turned out to be truly amazing. Most of these people, from all over the world, ended up becoming my good friends. It was incredible. Blackout poetry changed my life. It gave me a sense of belonging and purpose. Honestly, it SAVED my life. It enabled me to start over.

Reenergized, I decided that I wanted to shift my life focus to helping and encouraging others. I wanted to share my love for blackout poetry with everyone — most important, with those suffering from mental health illness or having just a rough time in general. That is what blackout poetry means to me. It is a vehicle of love passing on from one person to the next. It's about inspiring others and being inspired by others through art and words, and through finding stories of hope, love, and determination. When you get right down to it, it's therapy.

It's about finding light in the darkness.

I hope you're inspired by this book and that it reminds you that you can be as creative as you want. You have no limitations. I believe in you! Please join me on this journey and find out what blackout poetry can mean to you!

With much love,

MIKE

THIS IS ONLY
THE BEGINNING

THE FAITHFUL FRIEND

By MARIE SHEDLOCK

LONG ago, when Buddha-dhura was reigning in Benares, the Bodisat became his Minister. At that time a dog used to go to the state elephant's stable to feed on the lumps of rice where the elephant fed. Being attracted by the food, he came there often, and in time the dog and the elephant became great friends, and neither would eat without the other; and they took great delight in each other's company. At last the elephant's run-away keeper sold the dog to a countryman, who gave the elephant-keeper money for him and took him to his village. From that time the elephant, missing the dog, would neither eat nor drink, nor bathe. And they let the King know this. He sent the Bodisat, saying, "Go, wise Sir, and find out what's the cause of the elephant's behavior."

So he went to the elephant's stable, and seeing the elephant looked sad, said to himself, "There seems to be nothing the matter with him. He must have formed some close friendship, and now must be suffering from the loss of it." So he asked the elephant-keepers, "Is there anyone with whom he is particularly friendly?"

"Certainly, Sir! There is a dog of whom he was very fond, indeed."

"Where is it now?"

"Some man or other took it away."

"Do you know where the man lives?"

"No, Sir!"

Then the Bodisat went and told the King: "There's nothing the matter with the elephant, Your Majesty; but he was great friends with a dog, and I fancy it's through missing it that he refuses his food."

Great Lent begins (Or...

a collection of
blackout poetry and
other ramblings through
a journey of depression,
love, loss, life and
starting over.

I

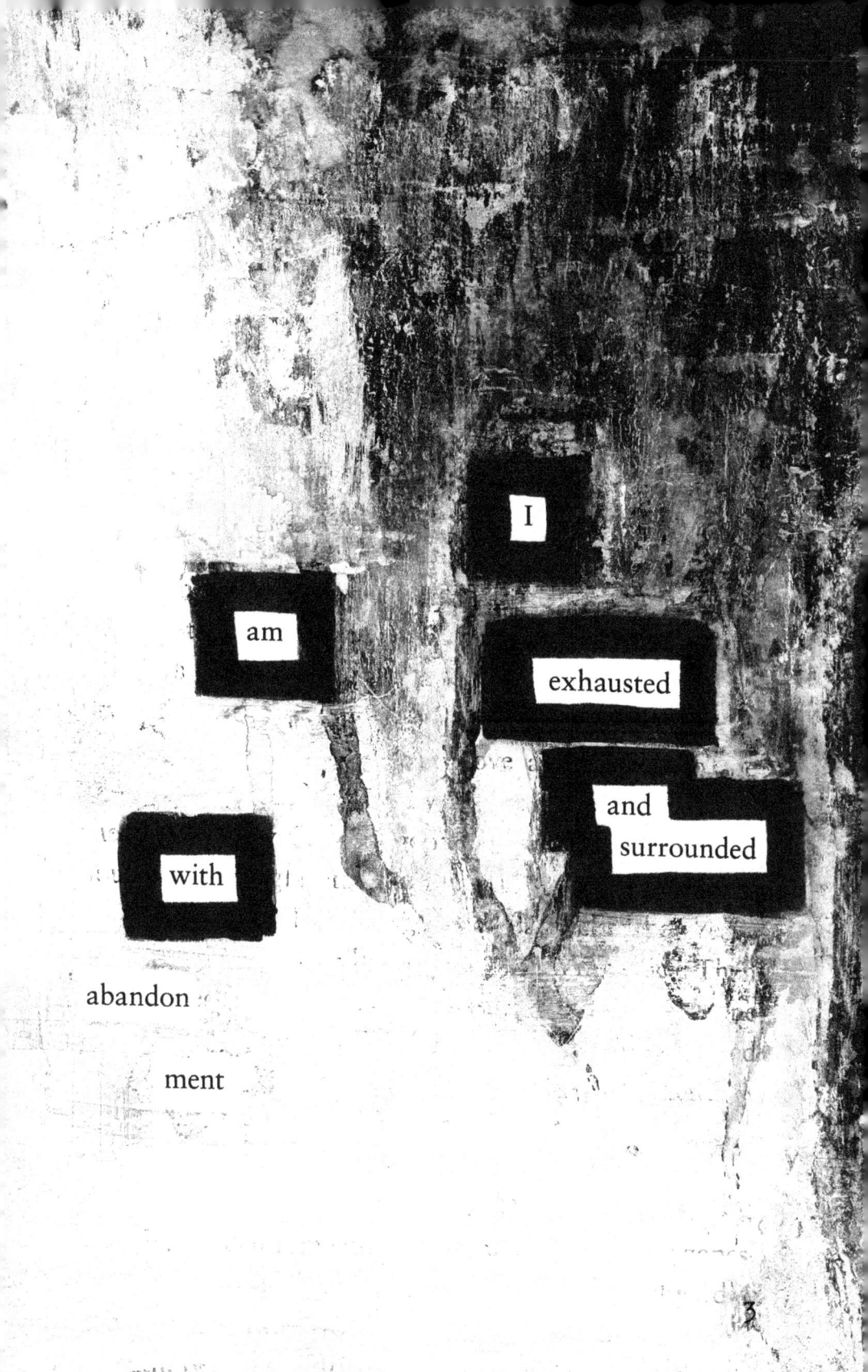

am

exhausted

and
surrounded

with

abandon

ment

the spirit of
Stories

live
for   ever

Listen to the words in your heart

a   n d

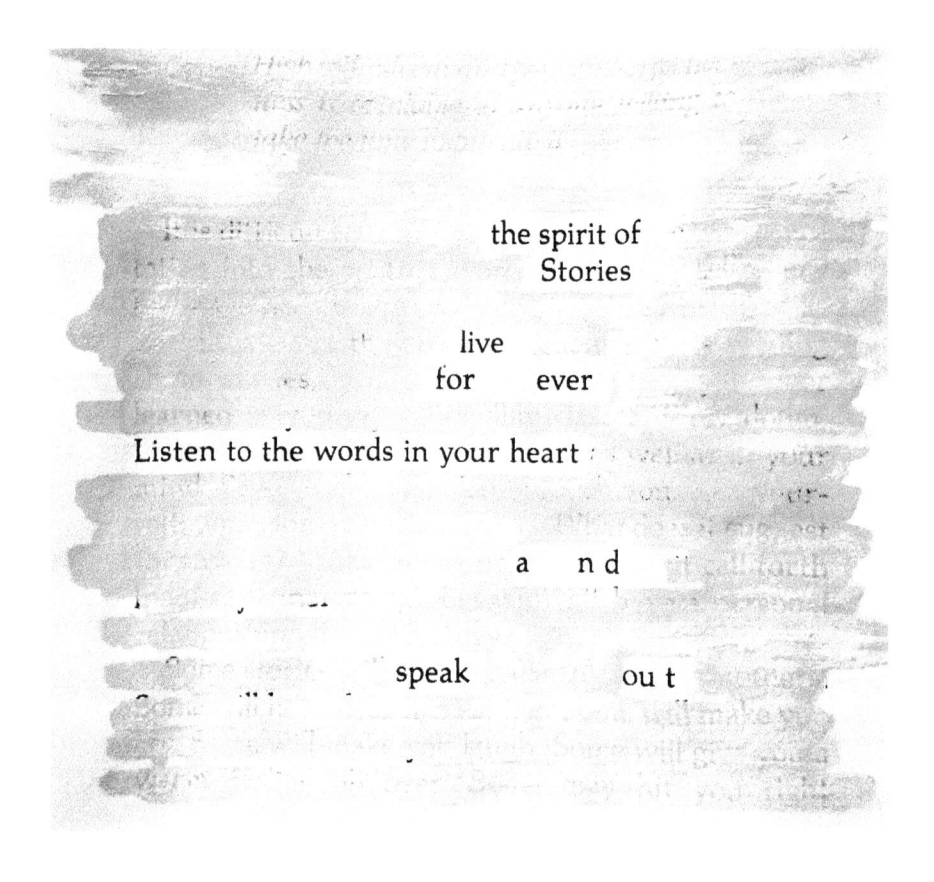

speak   ou t

Ghost Stories

Just Make Yourself Comfortable

important people count as miracles

For Joe

upon our final

dust and faded ink
I searched once again for
something that might indicate
the existence of

her   But there was no reference whatsoever

Disappearing Act

devilish

In the dark of night I lay in bed
As devils and demons dance through my head
And you cut in to join the dance
In my devilish dreams
Where I stand no chance

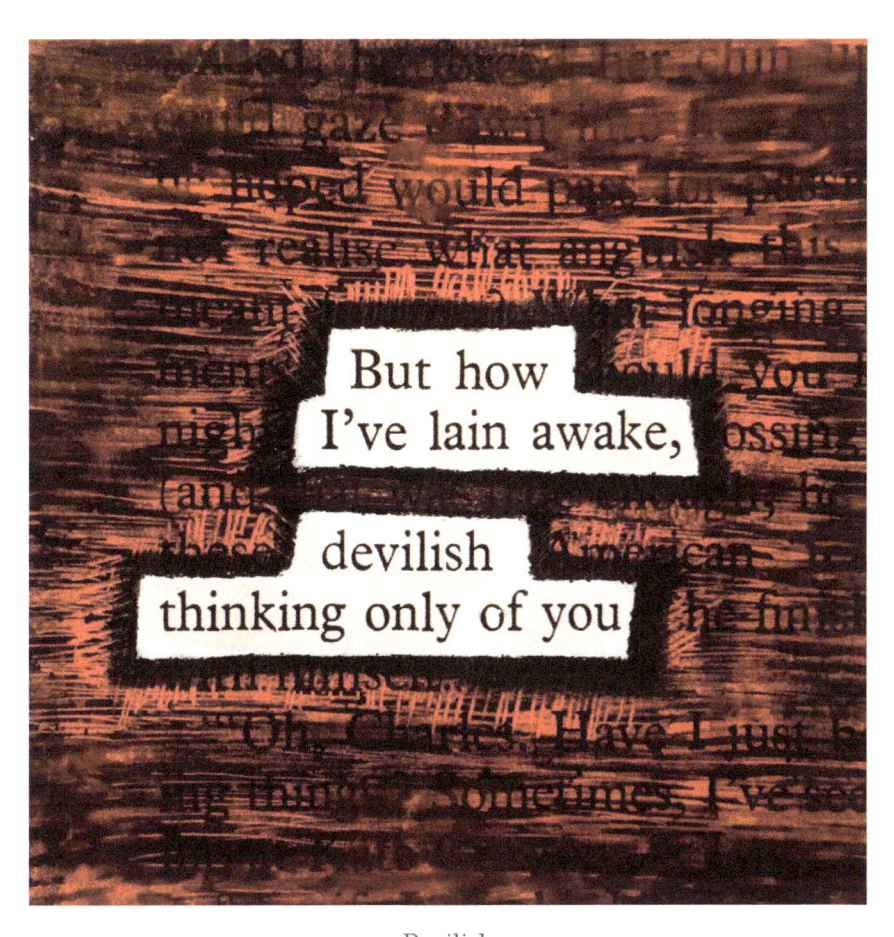

> But how
> I've lain awake,
> devilish
> thinking only of you

Devilish

Let It Go - A Tribute To E. E. Cummings

"You're amazing.

and

you

d o n t
even

know,

it

You're Amazing

This Is The Real Thing

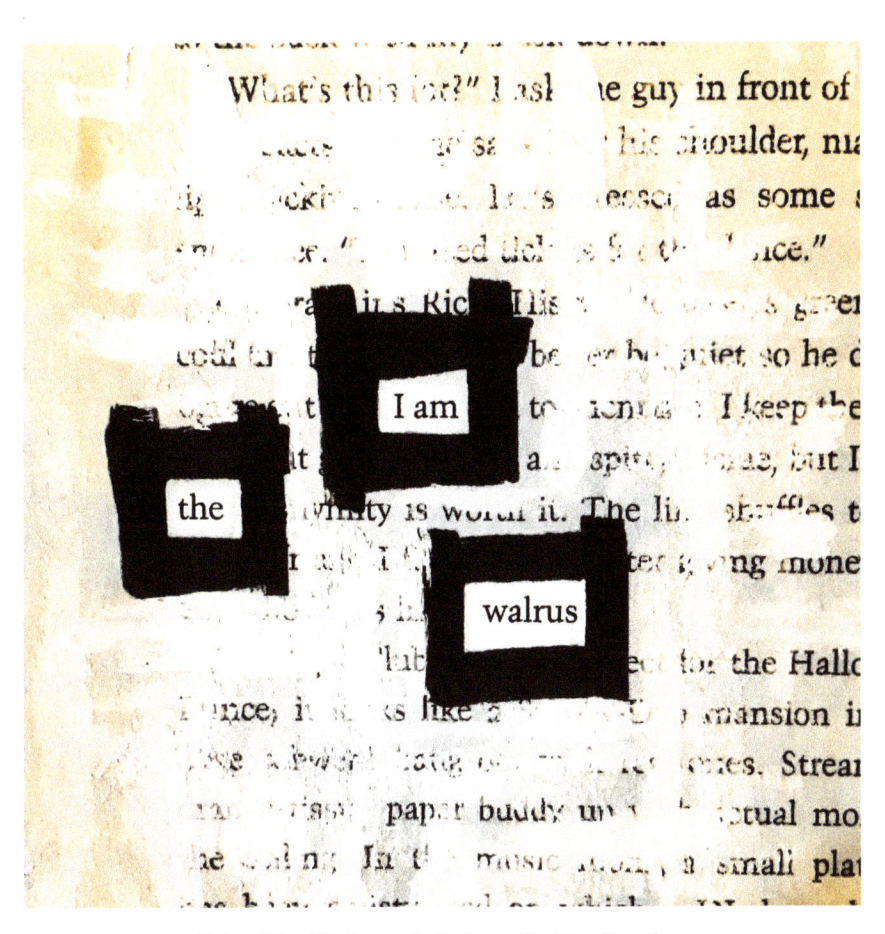

I Am The Walrus - A Tribute To The Beatles

nightmare

In darkest of hours the time that you crave
When muses awaken to come out and play
The dreamers, creators, the lost and alone
All shine in the darkness, give back of their souls
They don't mind the monsters hid under the bed
Or ones in the shadows that cower instead
For you are their nightmare, they're afraid of the dark
And all that flows through you, too brilliant a spark

But it's not 'til each morning, when you wake with such
dread, to go out and face what you know lies ahead

See, monsters are real and they thrive in the light
They follow your footsteps, with each one a fight
They'll bend you and twist you and get in your head
They'll tear at your insides and leave you half dead
Exhausted and weary, about to give in
Remember one thing as the dusk settles in
Stand tall and be brave at the last one you meet
Look it right in the eyes with a smile so sweet
Just whisper these words so soft and so light

Good evening, my friend. I'll see you tonight

Become The Fear

An ending is always

followed

by a

new beginning

If you

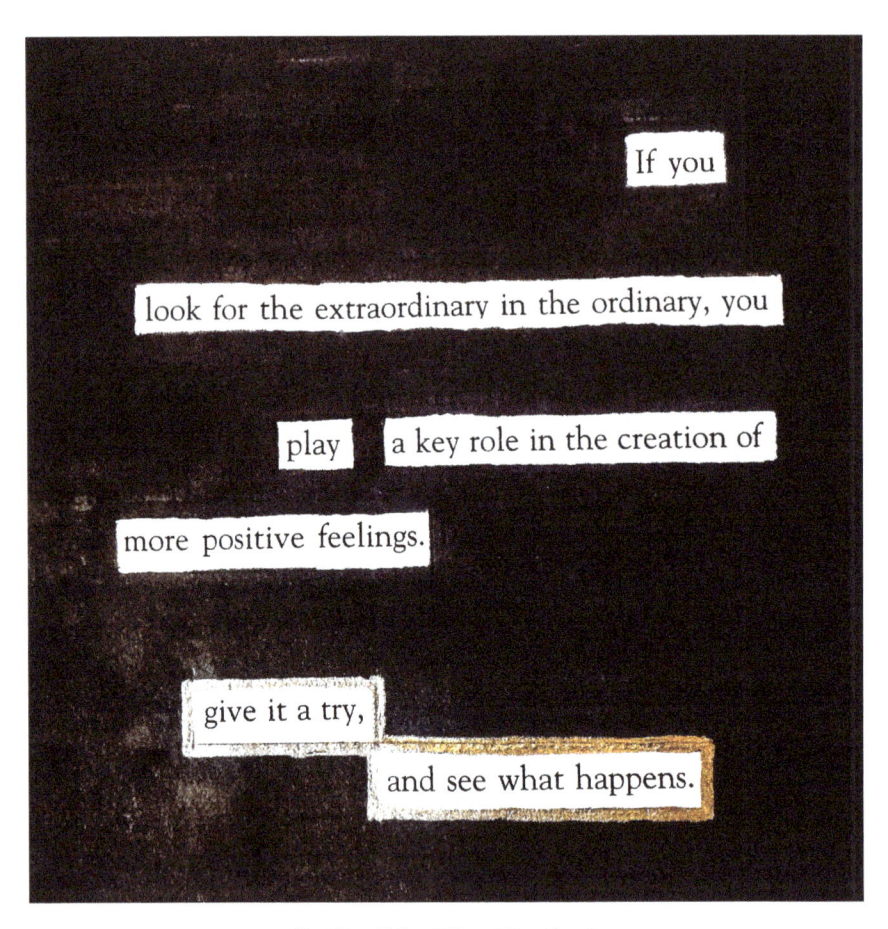

look for the extraordinary in the ordinary, you

play a key role in the creation of

more positive feelings.

give it a try,

and see what happens.

Do You Like What You See?

He will mourn forever on the edge of

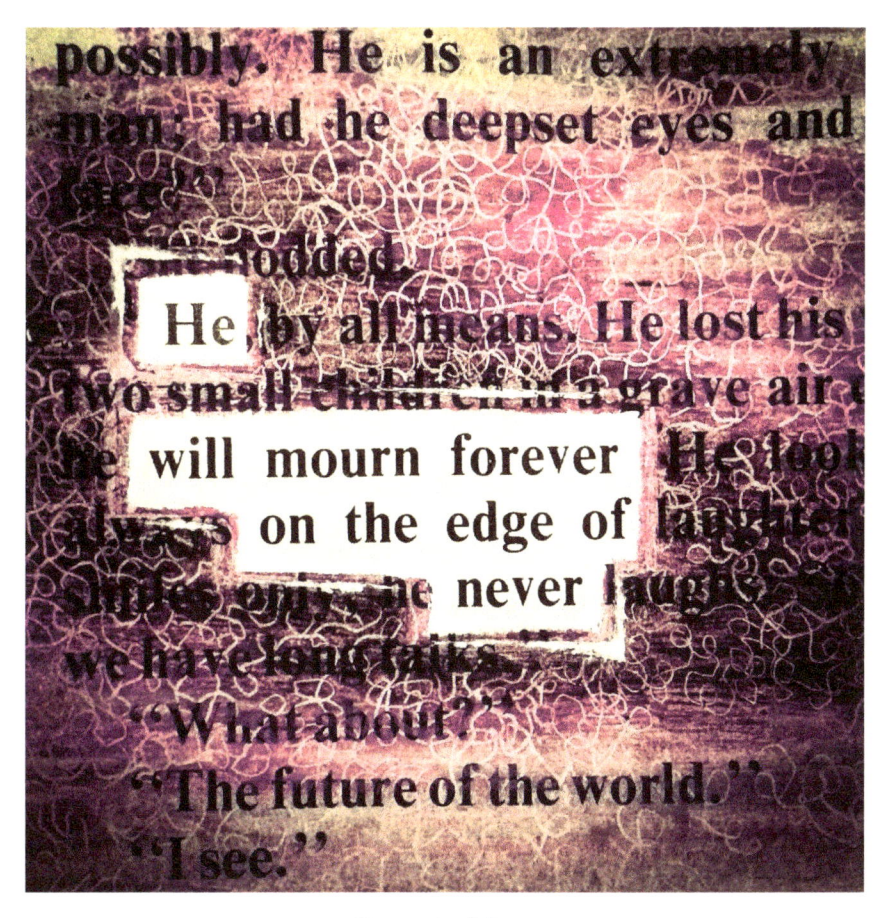

Unrequited Love

Michael's looking for a

"Redo"

"Trust me."

it's about to get good.

Make Over

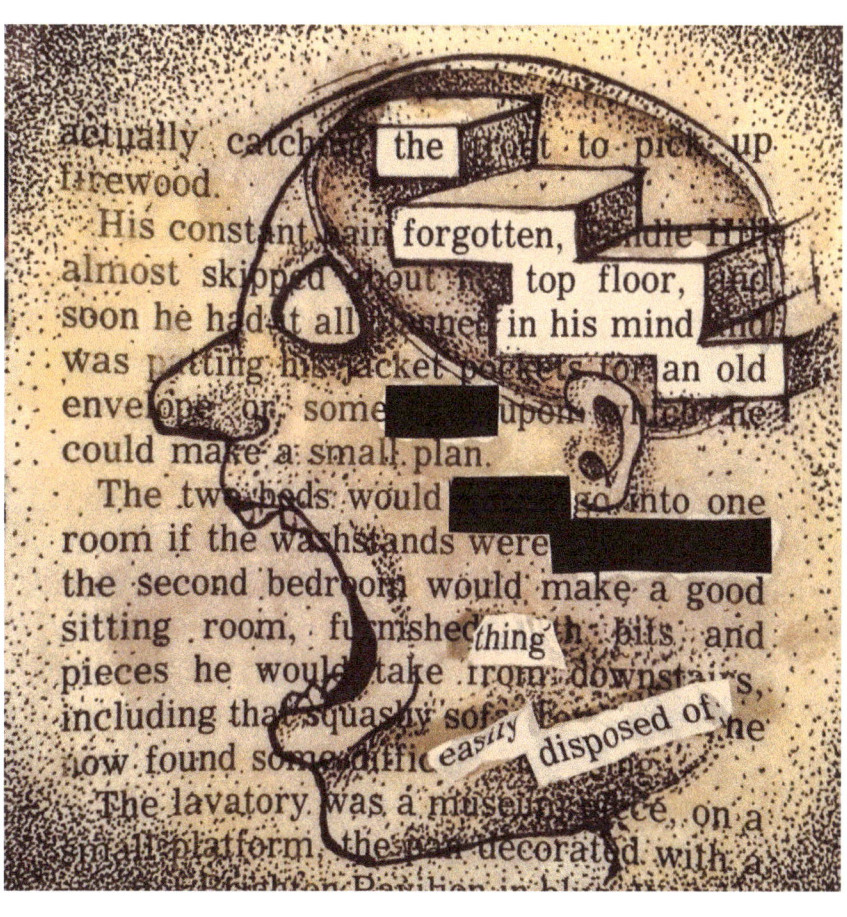

actually catch**the** t to pick up
firewood.
His constant **forgotten,** die Ho
almost skipped bout **top floor,**
soon he had t all **in his mind**
was p tting his jacket pocket **an old**
envelope or some upon which he
could make a small plan.
The two beds would so into one
room if the washstands were
the second bedroom would make a good
sitting room, furnished**thing** h bits and
pieces he would take from downstairs,
including that squashy sof **easily disposed of**
now found som difficulty
The lavatory was a museum piece, on a
small platform, the pan decorated with a

Things In The Attic

21

what you feel you
are, does not define
who you are.

– My Therapist

> Don't be less than yourself.

Confidence Is Key

Divine Epiphany

love is a naughty misdemeanour

Crimes Of The Heart

i 'll
cash
you
outside

How Bow Dat

Life Is Damn Strange

YOU'VE
T BE CRUE
Presley)
KIE PART
THE SOUND
HEARD
4 Best S
THAT
WONDERFUL
FEELING
LONG PLAYING
PLAY THIS RECORD
Je - sus, All
temp - ta - tions? Is there
v-y - la - den, Cumbered with load
a priv - i - lege
We should nev-er be
Pre - cious Sav-ior, still
'ry-thing to God in
it to the Lord in
it to the Lord in
STEREO
LP
O what pea - feit,
Can we fi
Do thy fri
pain we bear
sor-rows sh
ord in
RECORDS AL
BEST
farther.
STEREOPHONIC EQUIPMENT
EXCLUSIVE OFF
E7♯9(no3rd)
Selling Record Coll tions
OFFER! NOT AVAILABLE IN S RES ANYWH

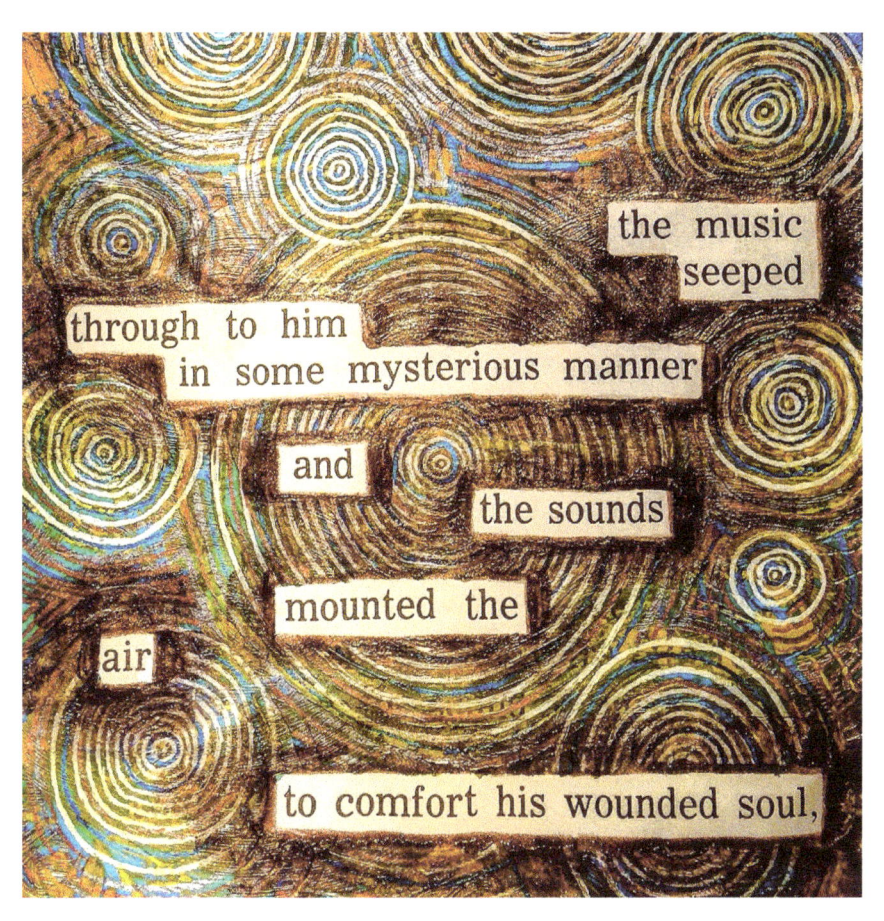

the music
seeped
through to him
in some mysterious manner
and
the sounds
mounted the
air

to comfort his wounded soul,

Music Is What Feelings Sound Like

                    her
         voice could be heard   and

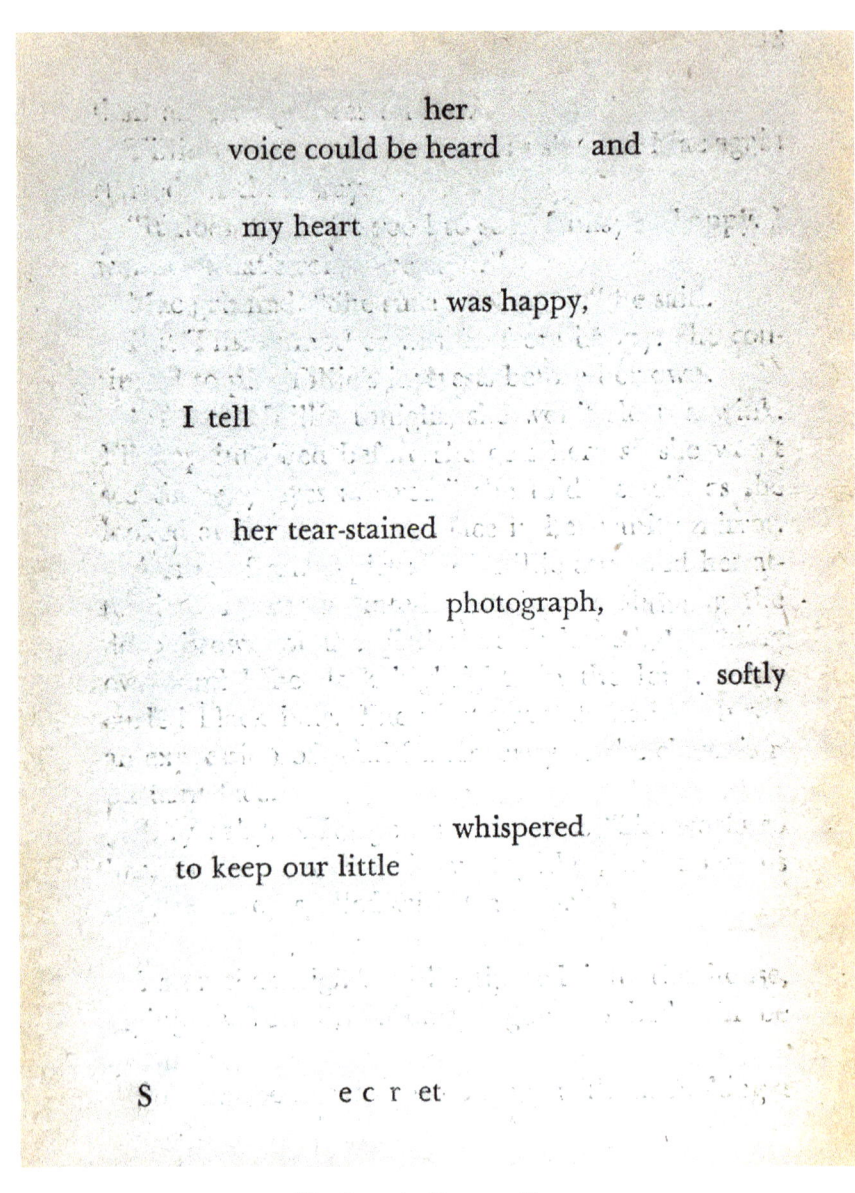

     my heart

                      was happy,

   I tell

       her tear-stained

                  photograph,

                                softly

                   whispered
  to keep our little

          S   e c r et

The Secret - Erasure Poem

in the future,
metaphysical music and
the consciousness of
reality.
was your old self.
My delight
trip was essentially the joy of
everything
she confronted
of her
never primped,
tied behind the neck,
casually fixed her hair
of her being.
that went on for miles,

Walk The Line for #bpchallenges

whatever
I think—

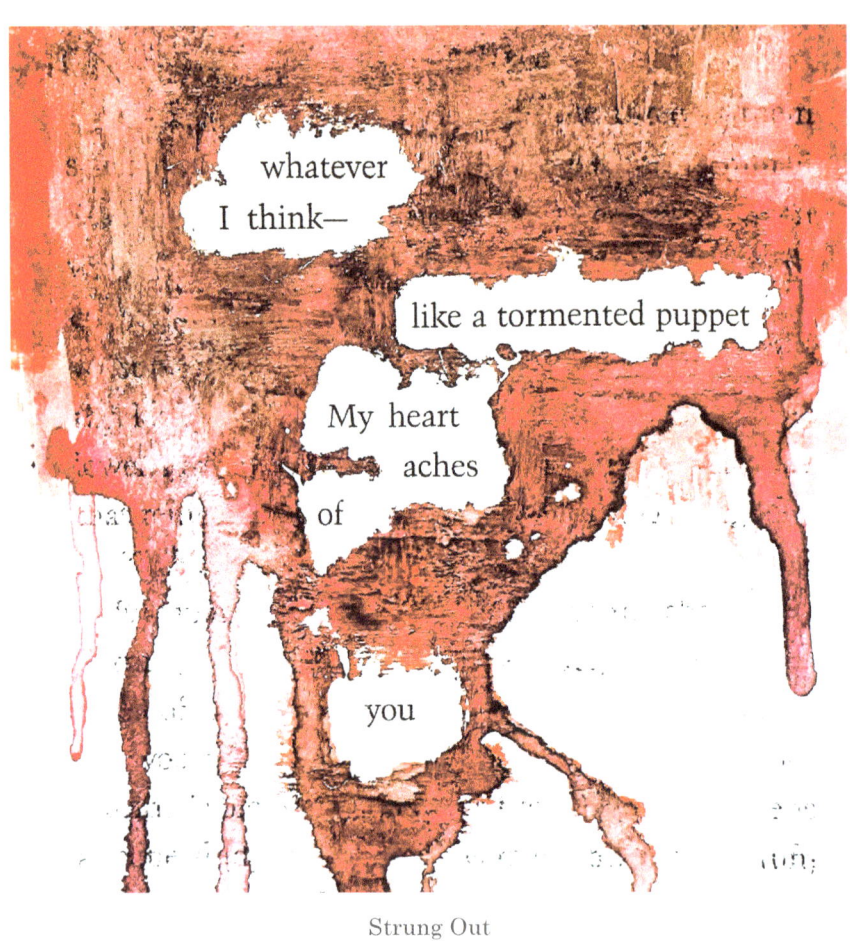

like a tormented puppet

My heart
aches

of

you

Strung Out

we decay
we reincarnate,
into
the branch of
a tree fighting for its life.

Circle Of Life

34

I Everything and feel nothing

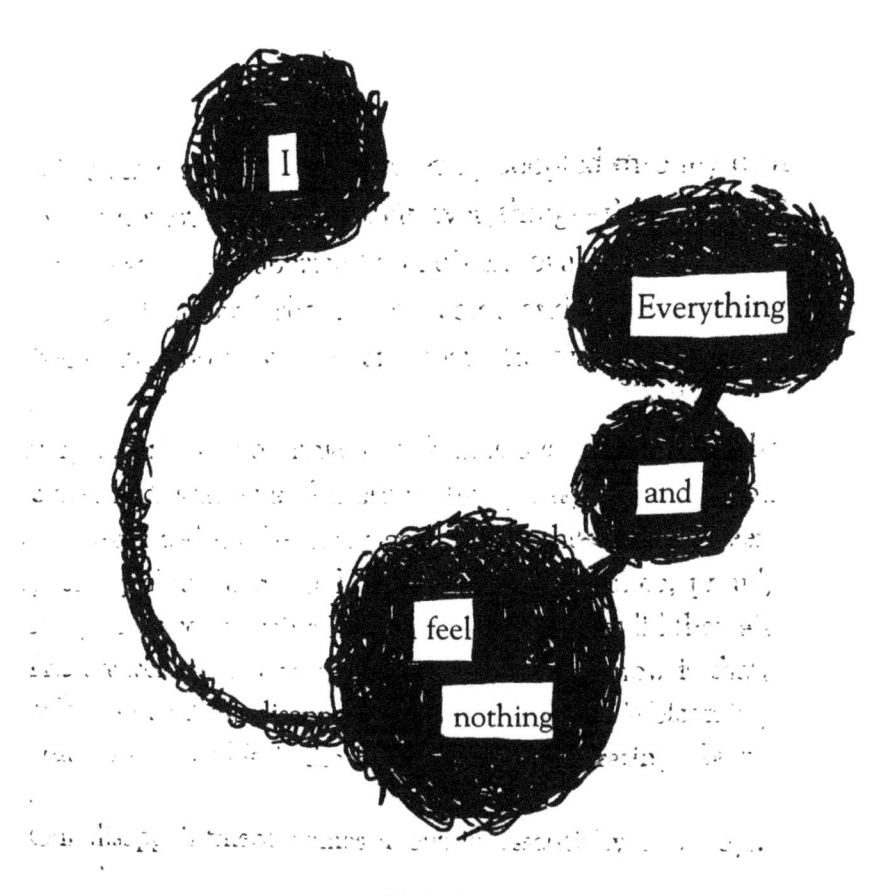

All At Once

ble traits by st........
persistence. When we......
has been war, there have also
have been plag..ed w........
As long as there was......
and other....er.che..........
as there was ig...ran...in the
teachers to help g....r..r to

These examples ...ught ..
own obstacles ....in..g th..
to rise above a..........W..
history, shape o.............
the other way a...un..

I believe that wh....l.....
evidence---whet....l. s.p
one in a concent......o..m..
executing tasks wi.. ..a. .e..
cause for celebr..........ll
remold a misshap............
living in dignity............

the human spirit can not be broken.

A semicolon is used when an author could've chosen to end their sentence, but chose not to. The author is you and the sentence is your life.

Michael is in a different dimension.

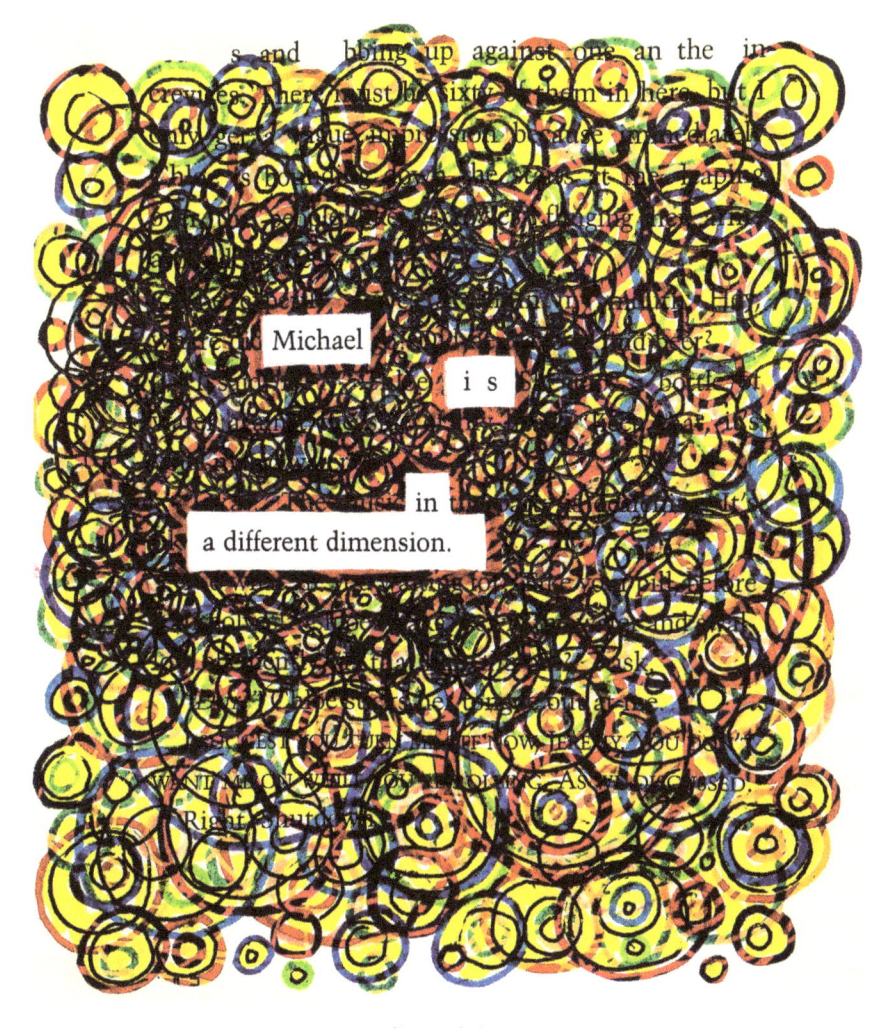

Spaced Out

There was a small silence—a distancing—as moment she was close, again. His heart stuttered heartbeats, waiting for her

The Distancing - Part One

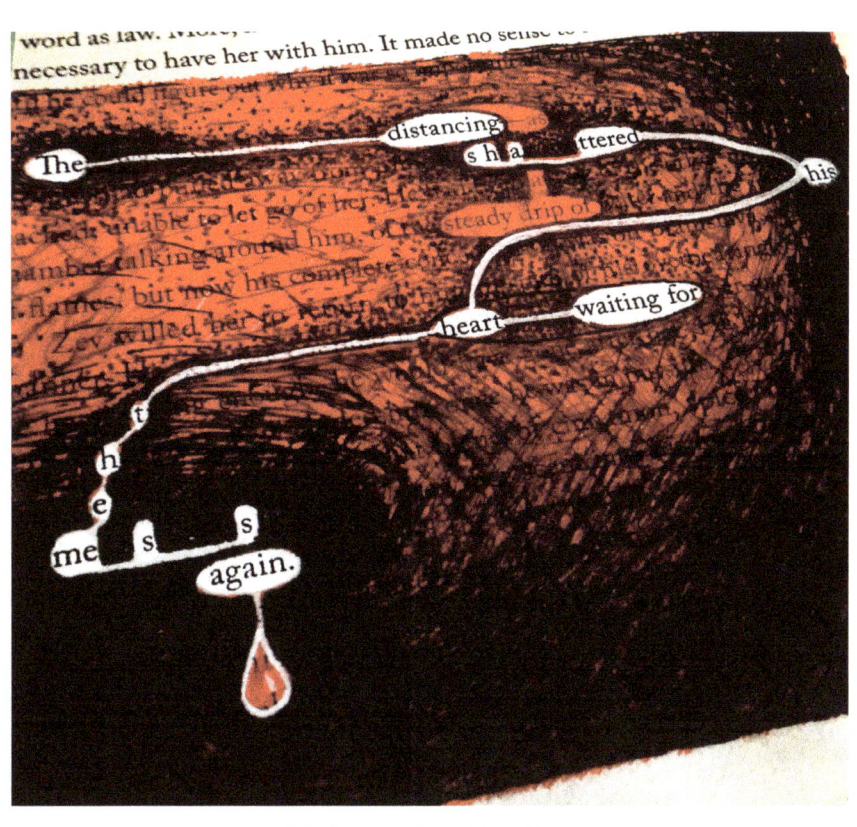

The Distancing — Part Two

it takes two to tango.
yet i am just one,
all twisted and tangled.

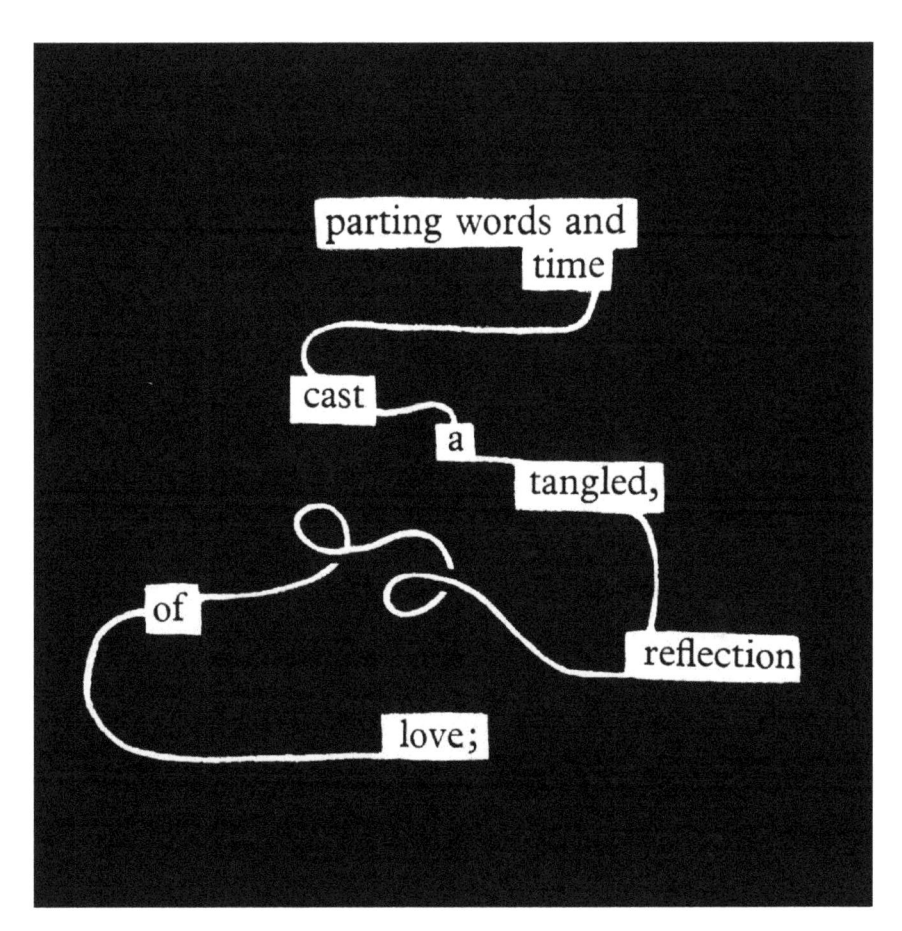

parting words and
time
cast
a
tangled,
of
reflection
love;

A Tangled Reflection Of Love

gives away your

heat

its

chilly outside

Projecting Warmth

floppy and laser discs make
Modern technology
complex.
we can't quite comprehend the
things we used to do
without machines. Like laughing.

we built the

u
n

human

Domo arigato, Mr. Roboto

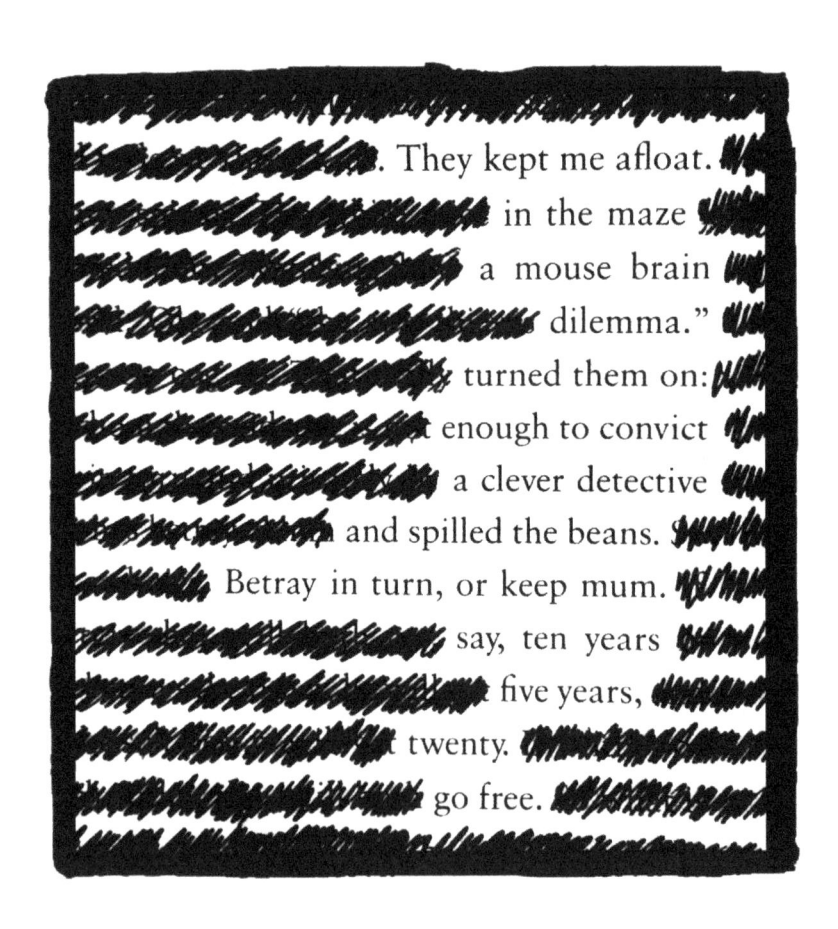

. They kept me afloat.
in the maze
a mouse brain
dilemma."
turned them on:
enough to convict
a clever detective
and spilled the beans.
Betray in turn, or keep mum.
say, ten years
five years,
twenty.
go free.

Walk The Line for #bpchallenges

searching for words **to** **leave** **out**

Lost For Words - Erasure Poem

you are my light on the darkest of nights

the darkness

seemed to be made of
Little fireflies
caught
in
the
air
the color
followed the curve
to
his heart

Fireflies

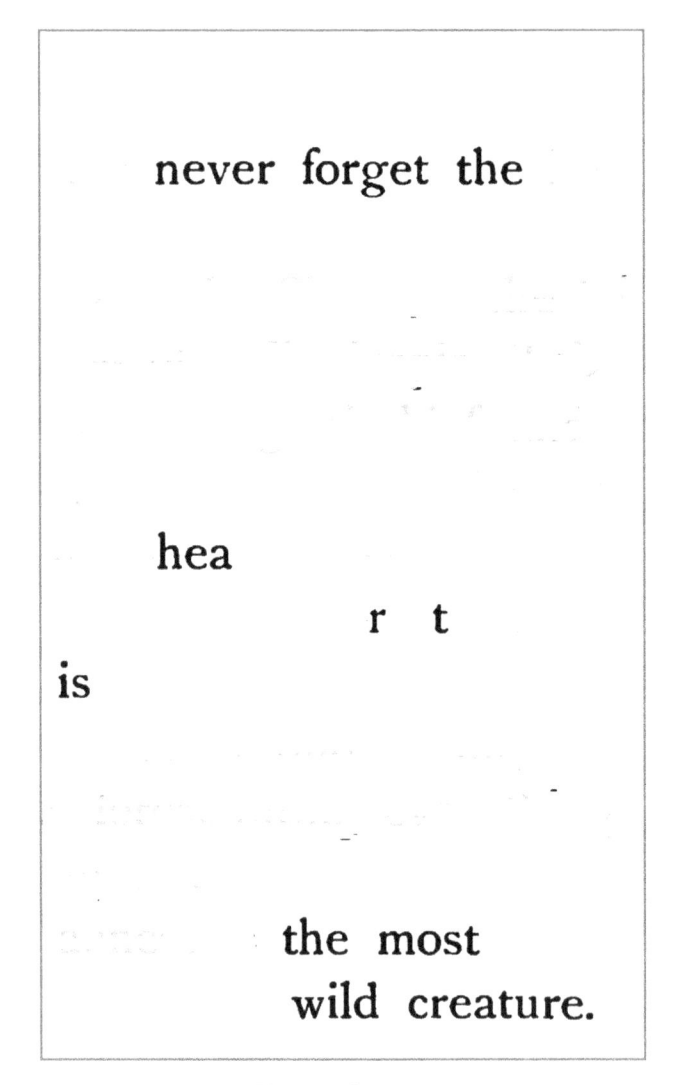

>   never forget the
>
>
>
>
>   hea
>   r   t
> is
>
>
>
>   the most
>   wild creature.

Untamed Heart

> Breathing hard, she clenched her eyes shut.
>
> They hung around anyway, Everyone standing around looking
>
> . It's not like the rest of it.
> The rest of it that had once been

Social Anxiety

Night Vision - Lights On
(Created with glow in the dark acrylic paint)

Night Vision - Lights Off
(Created with glow in the dark acrylic paint)

laughter is a powerful prescription for just about anything. it can change your mood from bad to good in just a few seconds. it can remind you not to take life too seriously. make sure you get a full dose of laughter every single day. watch a funny movie. spend some time laughing with your friends and family. laugh at yourself. laugh out loud when you are by yourself. but most of all, make other people laugh, because that is truly one of the greatest gifts you can give to another person.

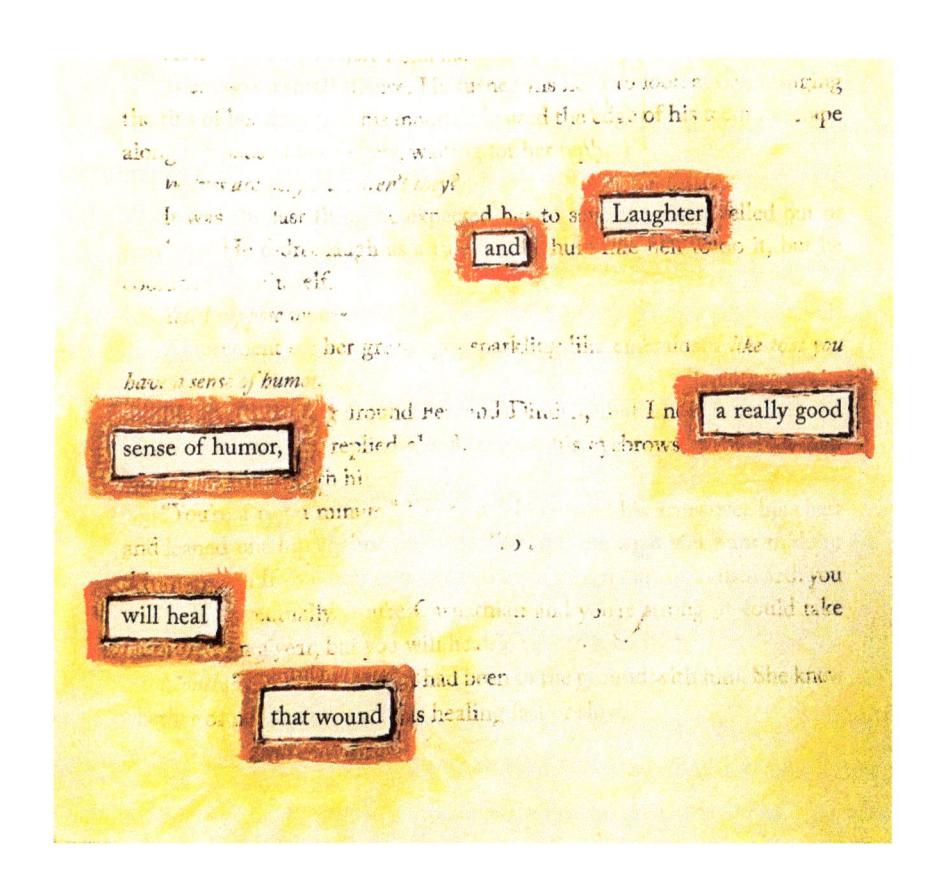

Laughter and sense of humor, a really good will heal that wound

Laughter Is Good For The Soul

still the

same person I've always been

plant hope to expect success.

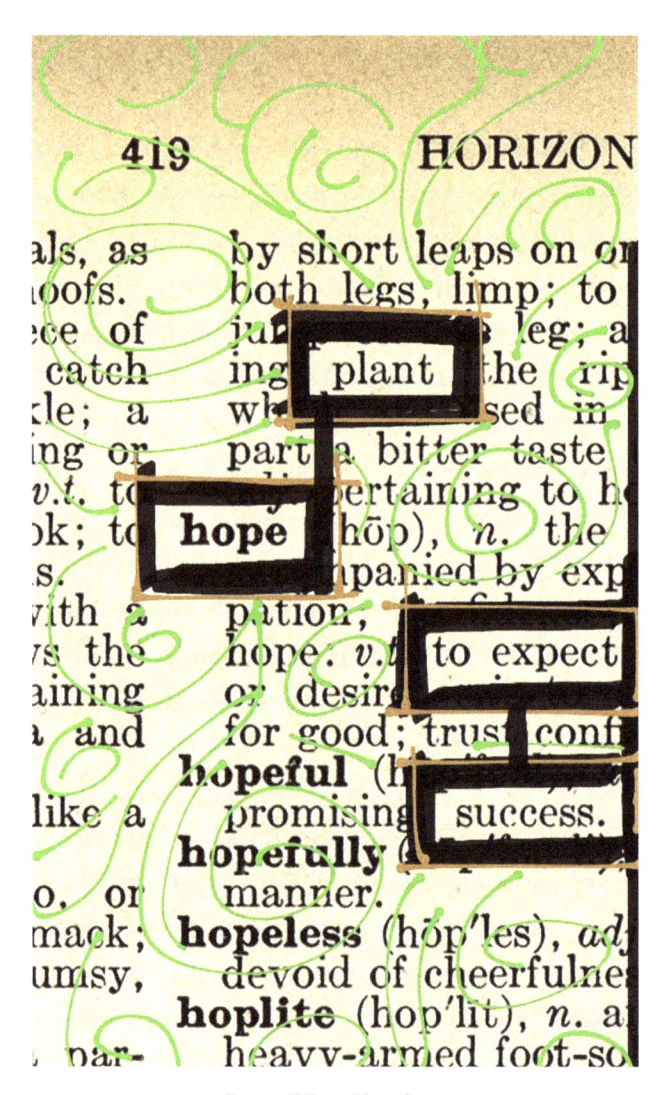

Reap What You Sow

how deep a longing,

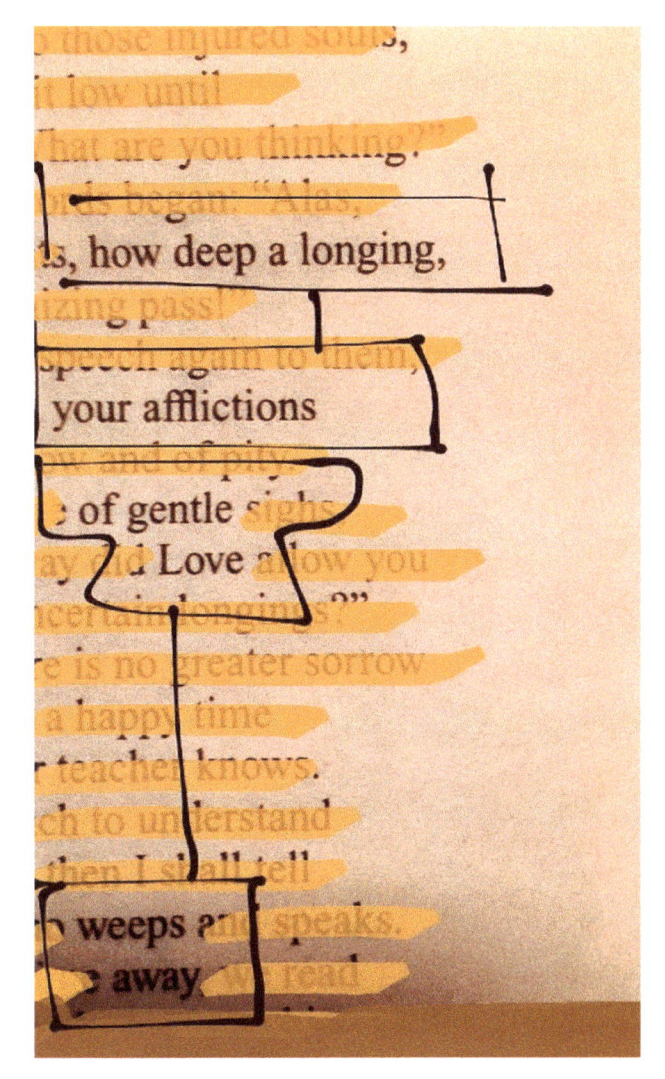

your afflictions

of gentle
Love

weeps
away

Healing Love

the future is unknown,

be ready

now

Nothing Is Certain

you're not dreaming. You are beginning *rebirth.*

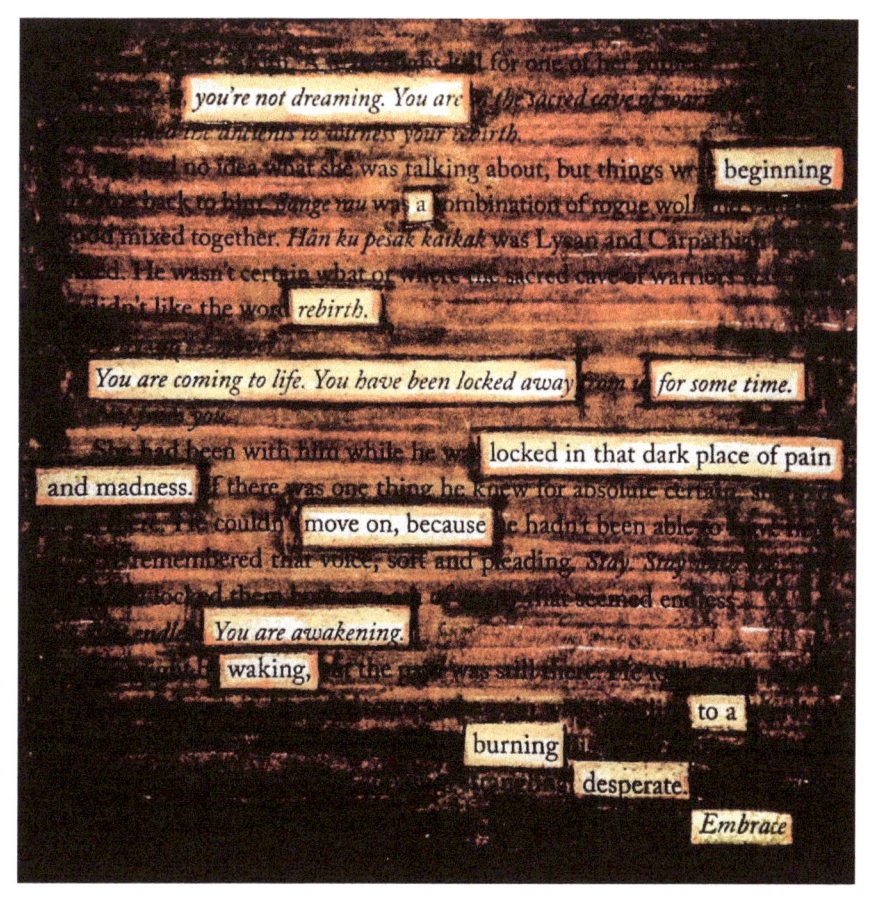

You are coming to life. You have been locked away *for some time.*

locked in that dark place of pain and madness. move on, because

You are awakening. waking, to a burning desperate. *Embrace*

Rebirth

having a mental illness is absolutely terrifying. youre fighting a constant battle in your mind every day. feelings of loneliness, rejection, self-doubt, shame...thats only the tip of the iceberg. and many people around you, including your closest friends and family, probably dont really understand what youre going through. im here to tell you that everything is going to be okay. you are stronger than most people out there. you got this. you are not alone. i believe in you. now its time to start believing in yourself. you are not the byproduct of your illness. you have the power to control this chapter in your life. remember that. one chapter in the entire book of your life. so keep on going, because youre going to have one hell of a story to tell.

Mental Health Awareness Series #1

63

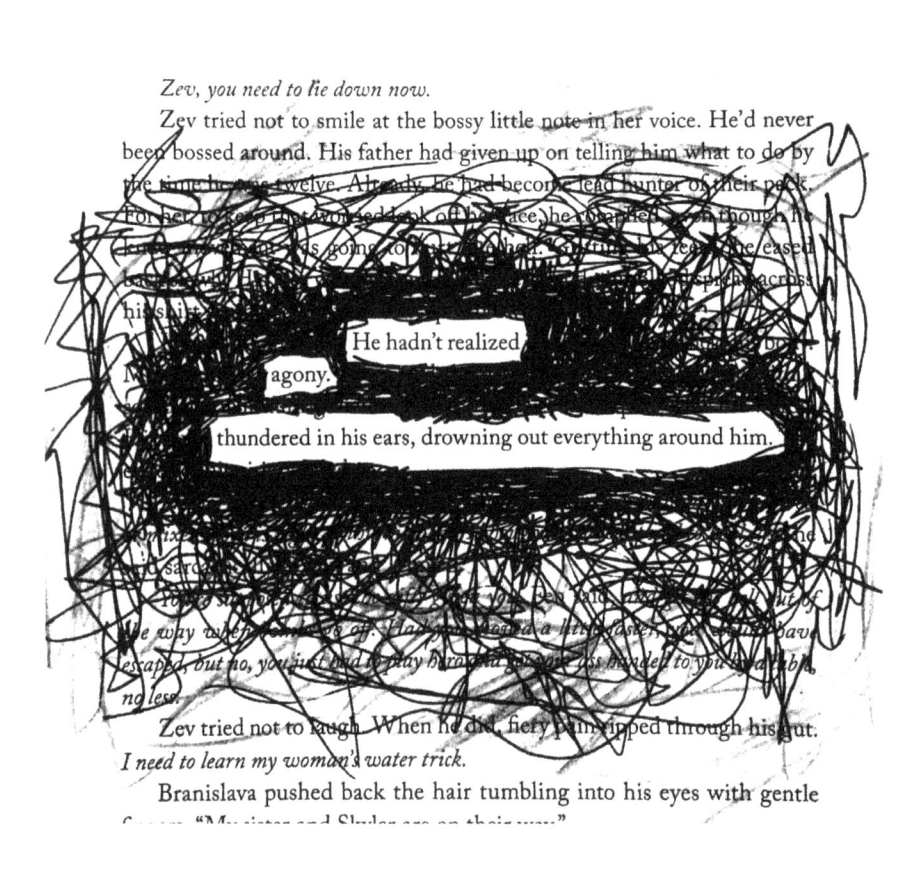

Zev, you need to lie down now.

Zev tried not to smile at the bossy little note in her voice. He'd never been bossed around. His father had given up on telling him what to do by the time he was twelve. Already he had become lead hunter of their pack.

He hadn't realized

agony.

thundered in his ears, drowning out everything around him.

Zev tried not to laugh. When he did, fiery pain ripped through his gut.
I need to learn my woman's water trick.

Branislava pushed back the hair tumbling into his eyes with gentle

Mental Health Awareness Series #2

important as figuring out who our enemy truly is. Zev is the person who can do that."

"The council members are friends," Zev said. "I've spent my life protecting them and enforcing their laws. I can't just switch sides." He ran his hand through his hair. It was thick and long, untamed and hanging around his face

his head.

was

all over the place

bordering on being out of control

Mental Health Awareness Series #3

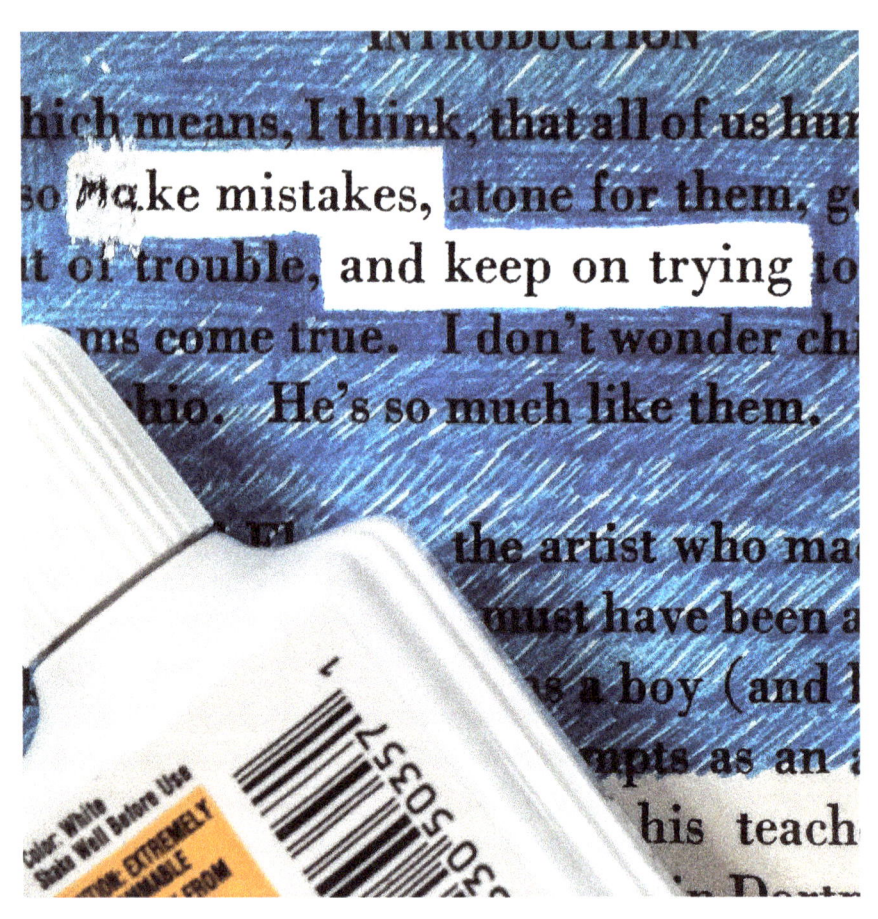

Even Mistakes Mean We're Trying

Two ships passing,

for now,

Your true love.

hope   holds
out   or
   chance,   This one won't

hold
water

Hope Floats

namaste

"My soul honors your soul.
I honor the place in you where
the entire Universe resides.
I honor the light, love, truth,
beauty and peace within you,
because it is also within me.
In sharing these things
we are united, we are the same,
we are one."

The colors of His soul filled every detail of his veins at once and swirled into heart.s mingling their one, union in

Swirled In Union

69

we

were   seeking

The
    One thing they *didn't* have

as
      We wrap our bodies in

improvised.

precaution

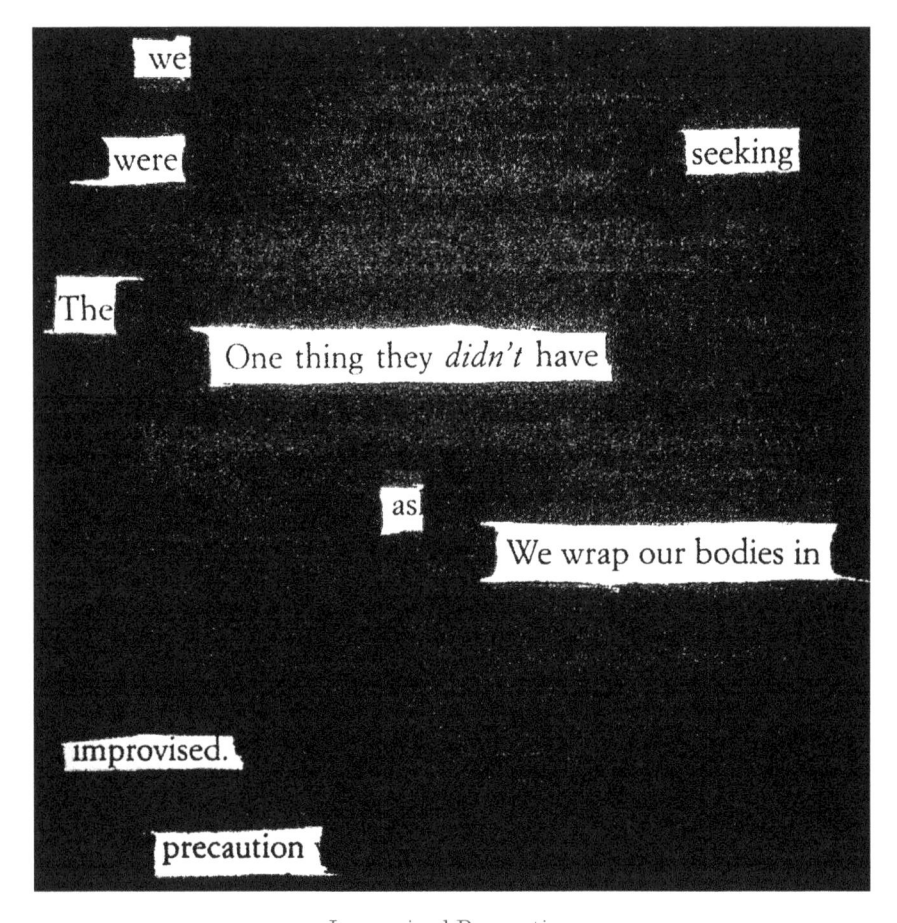

Improvised Precaution

love is

prone to

loneliness

Vulnerability

Fall in love with
the person
y ou
can always
be
and
you'll see
your life
Flow

In The Flow

These remnants were   Silvery white,
sunlight.

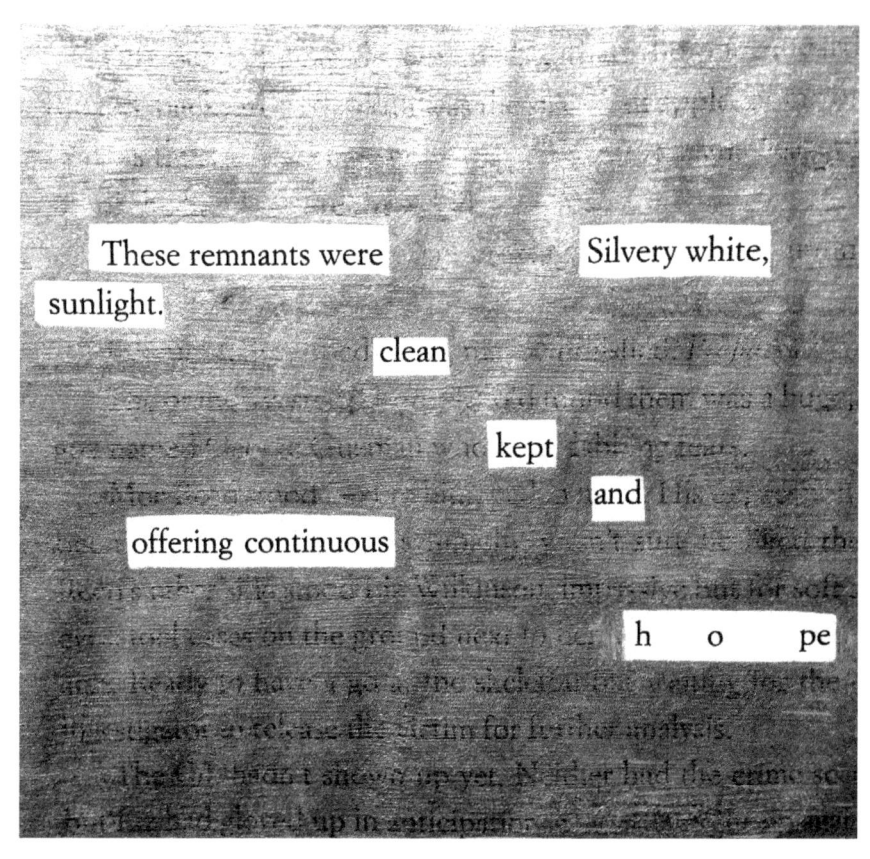

        clean

             kept
                and

offering continuous

                 h o pe

Remnants Of Hope

absolute value

You feel your days are numbered
All good things in the past
And factored in the bad times too
And thought they'd always last
You've looked at every angle
Divided where you stand
And tried to solve the problems
Subtracting where you can

But the point of the equation
Is not where you have been
But all the lessons you have learned
Both time and time again
And although it's a process
Don't rule out what's ahead
Keep adding to your timeline
And make it count instead
For really there's no formula
Or process to your plan
Just value where you're going
Reflect where you began

To sum it up one thing remains
That's absolute and true
One thing is always constant
And that constant is you

You Got This

have
as much
unconditional love

your pets as

Love is work in progress.

Labor Of Love

> eyes are red
>
> "Sorry," I say
>
> That was over

3x3x3 Blackout Poem for #bpchallenges

> when you
> create
> your soul stirs
> some   cosmic artist
> and
> you   feel
> the human *spirit—*

Cosmic Artist - Fibonacci poem which is six lines with a
syllable count of 1/1/2/3/5/8

never heard from you again.

you

right,

we got close
but never

wrote

the beautiful

poems

we know

Unpublished Love

the rioting heart

Deep within my hollow chest
A rioting heart won't let me be
The clawing
Gnashing
Beating
Bleeding
Pleading of a heart
That must break free

This tortured beast
Is pounding louder
Rattling
Tumbling
In its well worn cage
But will calm just slightly
And slow it's beating
When told a tale from
A timeless age

The one about a love
so true that's forged into the shape
Of a golden key
Stay calm dear heart
For when it's found
I'll swallow it whole
and set you free

Pop-Out Poetry Haiku

the tiger   s

           wi
                ll

        no   T

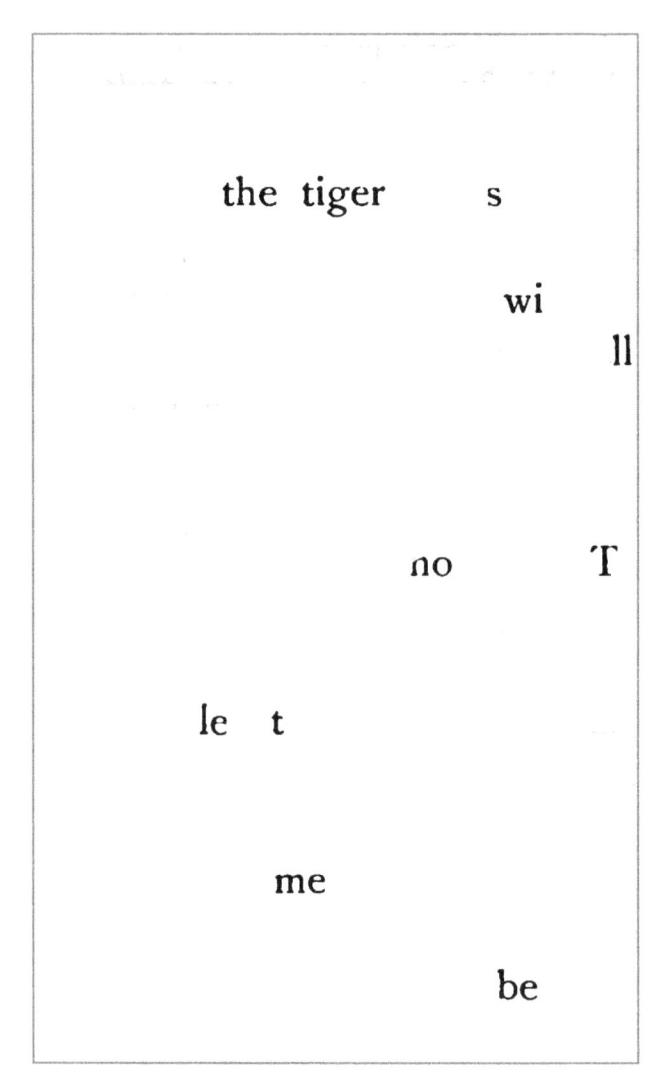

le   t

   me

          be

Tigers - A Tribute To Charles Bukowski

Happy Accident

On my altar with all the other icons
You were

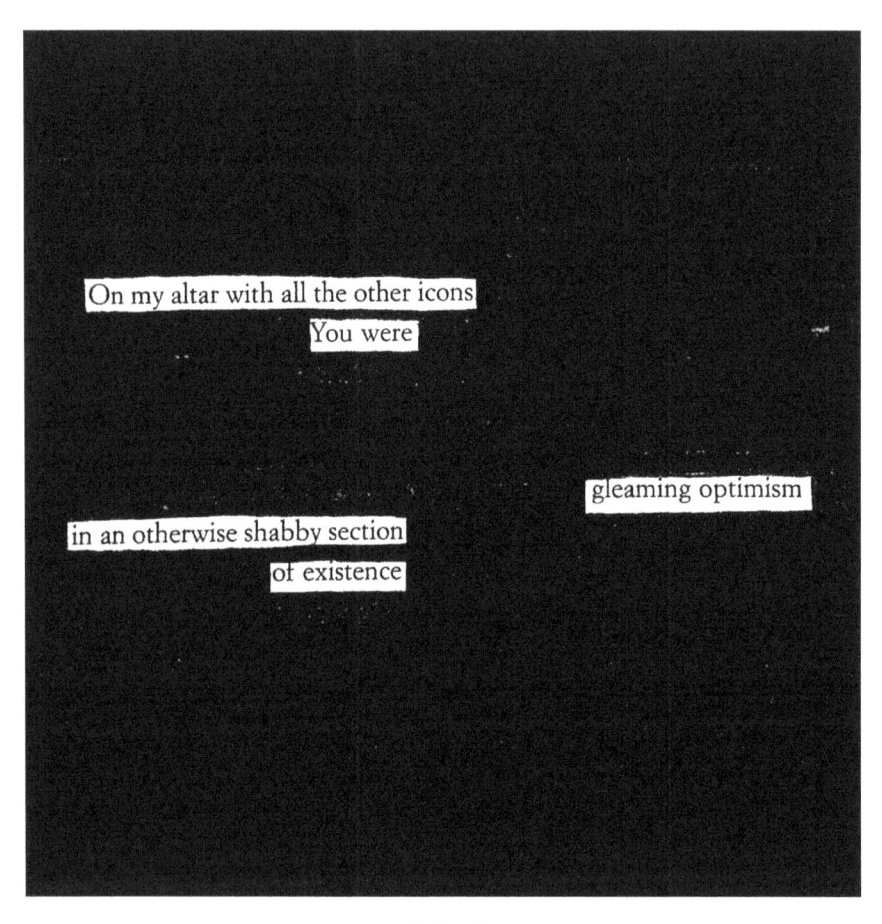

gleaming optimism

in an otherwise shabby section
of existence

Idol Shades

I Am An Island - A Tribute To Simon & Garfunkel

it is by chance that we met, by choice that we became friends.

– Unknown

helped to change many lives,

a beautiful

you

have

true

friend

Letter To A Friend

89

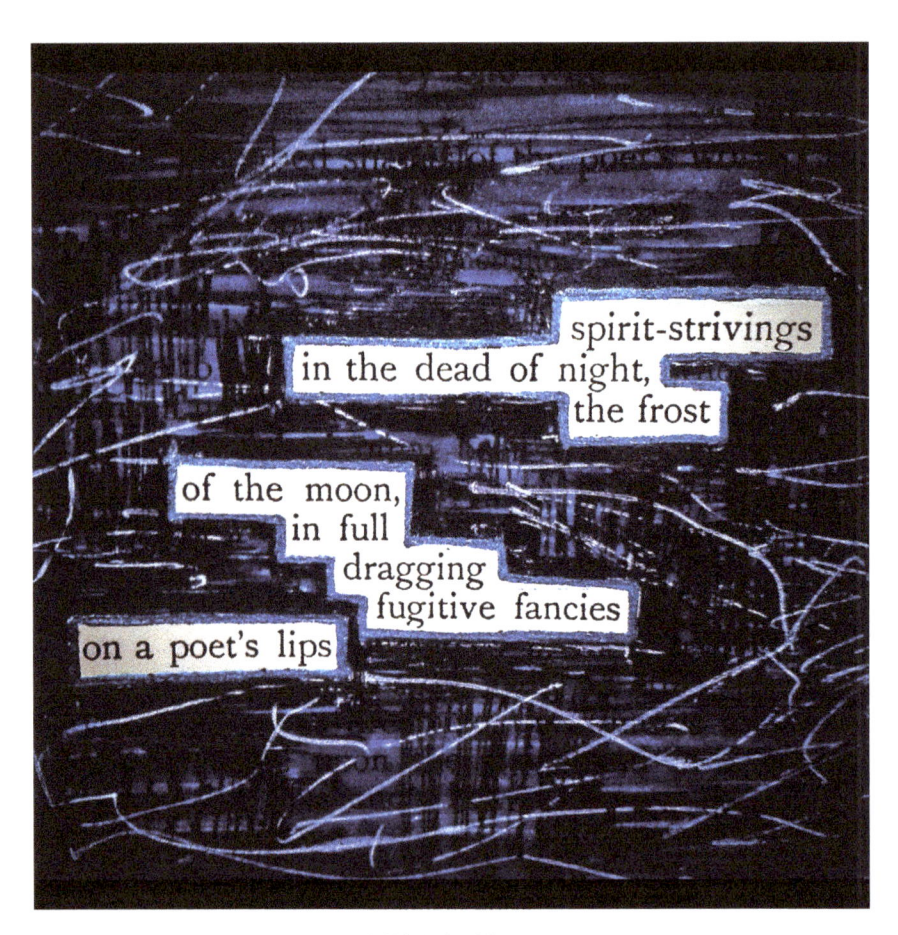

> spirit-strivings
> in the dead of night,
> the frost
> of the moon,
> in full
> dragging
> fugitive fancies
> on a poet's lips

Midnight Muse

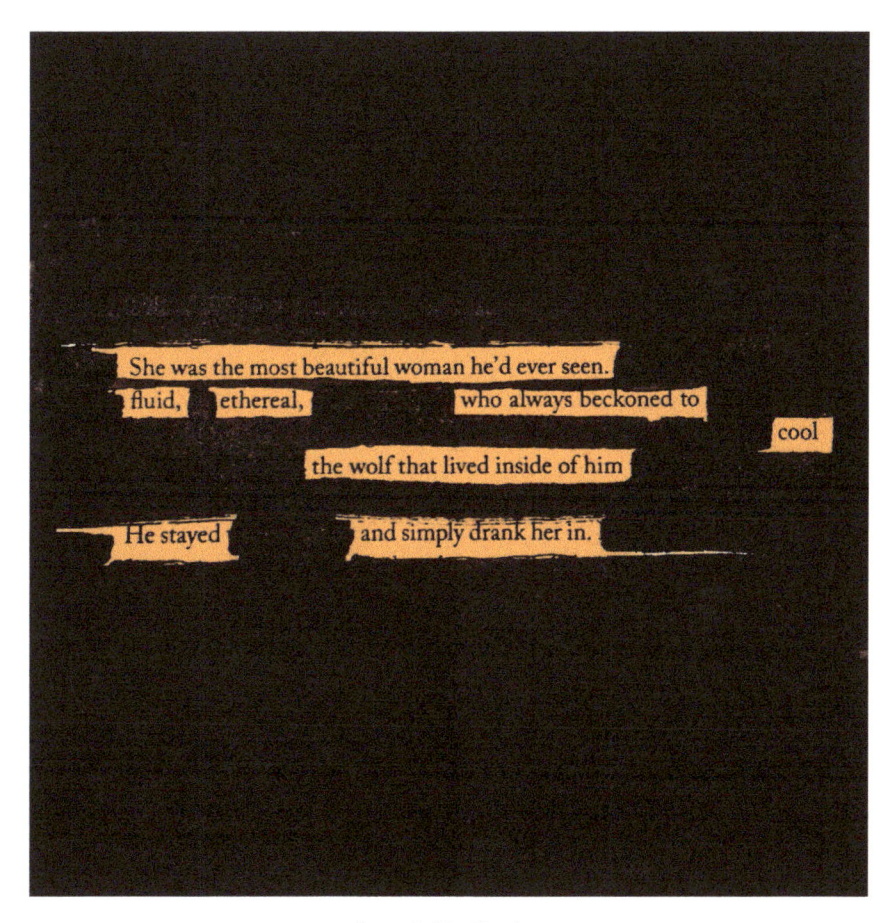

She was the most beautiful woman he'd ever seen.
fluid,   ethereal,   who always beckoned to
                                                    cool
the wolf that lived inside of him

He stayed   and simply drank her in.

Insatiable Desire

the half-moon of
her
heart
is surrealistic
and we
claw over each other

composed ye wild

Angelical Fiends

Be The Story

94

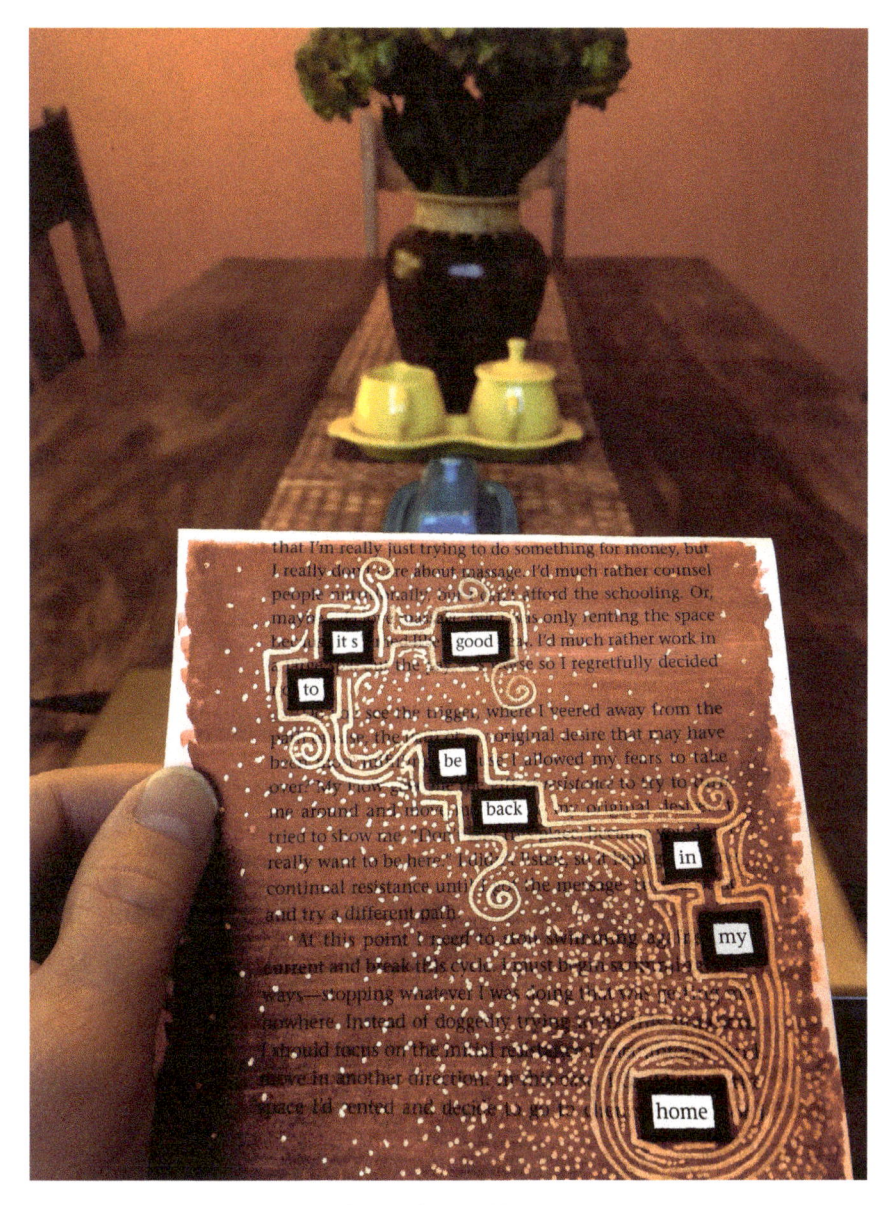

Home Sweet Home

Love

AND i just kept
going

hurts

penetrating blue eyes

casting

ice

Icy Stare

Bleeding Ink

my

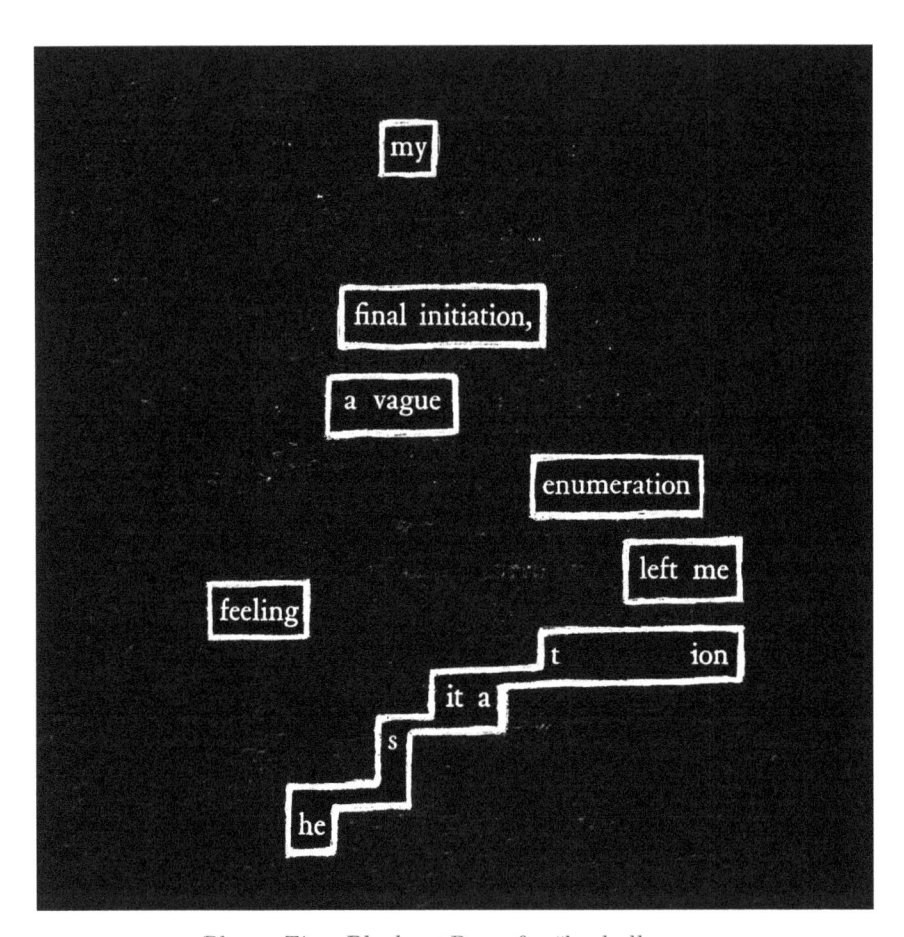

final initiation,
a vague

enumeration
left me
feeling
t   ion
it a
s
he

Rhyme Time Blackout Poem for #bpchallenges

Love Is A Madness That Has No Cure

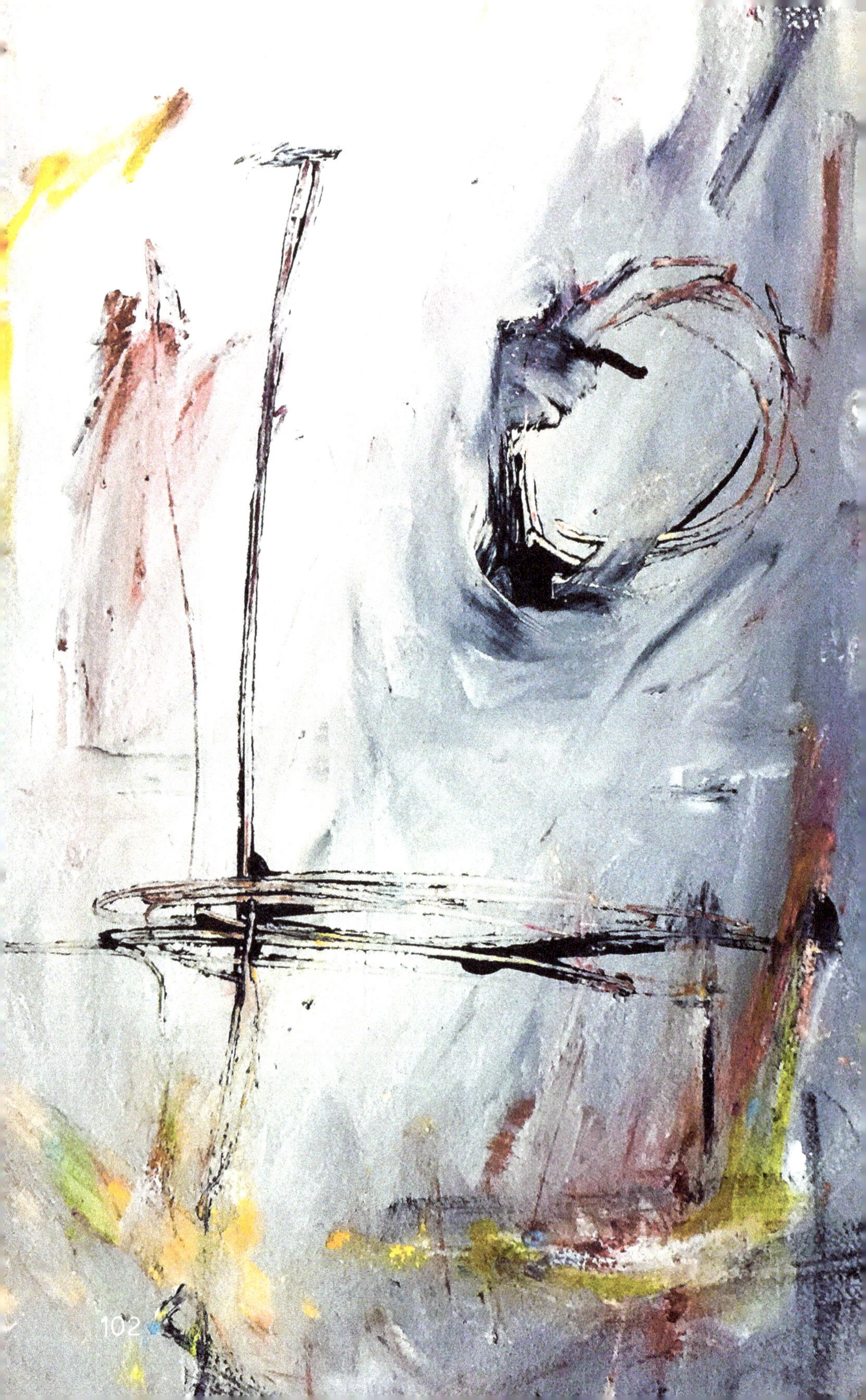

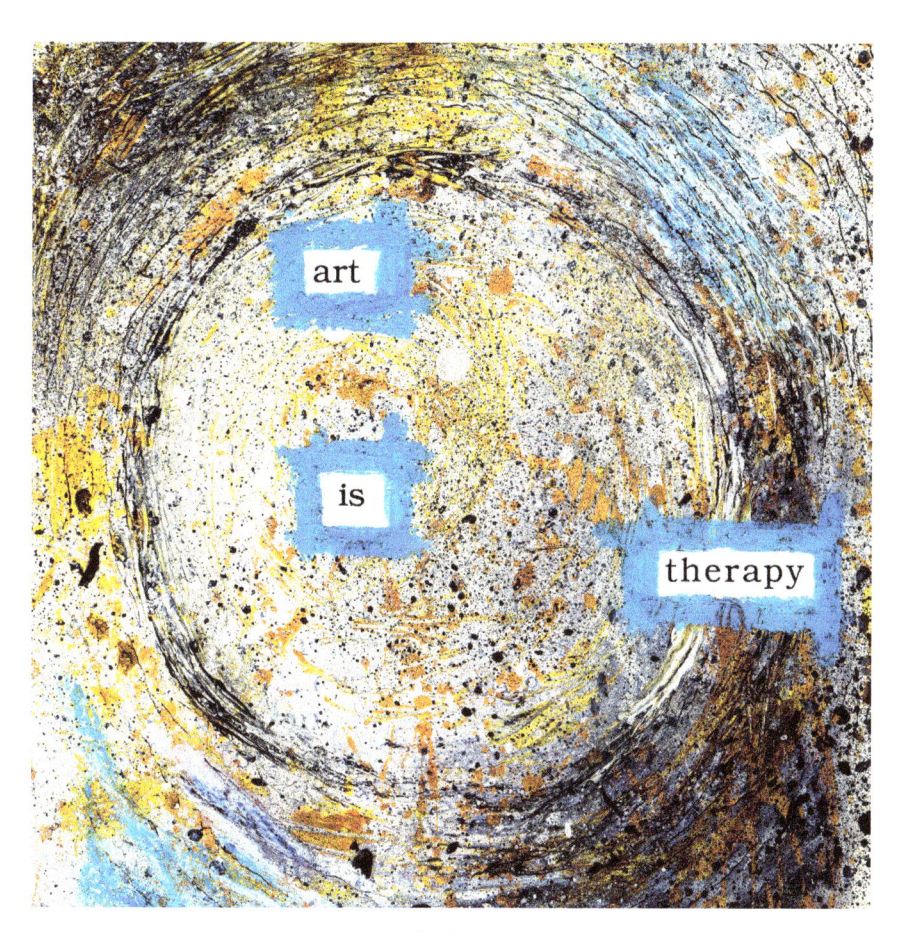

Art Is Therapy

good things destined to be planted over and over. in one particular place, I have a story to tell

Perennial Narrative

. It was the perfect place
so secret, so safe...

hiding right there

in her

he   a   r t

Comfort Zone

A Scar Means You Survived

What A Circus - A Tribute To Charles Bukowski

unconditional love

love is all we have

> ...you. I know that...
> ...be proved to be s...
> Please believe me...
> be faced together...
> now you are inn...
> ccused. We will...
> believe in you and...
> So please, *pleas*...

Love Is All We Have When There Is Nothing Else Left

                        swallowed up by

this paradise

                so beautiful

                        inside of

her

lips curving in a smile.

Swallowed Up By Hope - Part One

It was as though my soul
            finally
                smiled again, tears forming

                with

    ho   p
                e

Swallowed Up By Hope - Part Two

)dy suddenly seemed starved. He hadn't even kno
nt. He knew that ~~~~~~~~~~ had come r
e to gi~~~~~~~~~~~~~~~~~~~~~~~tain the
ces~~~~~~~~~~~~~~~~~~~~~~~~~~~feel e

surprise was a neat trick

Don't think it. Don't say it. Don't put it out into t.

Surprise Was A Neat Trick

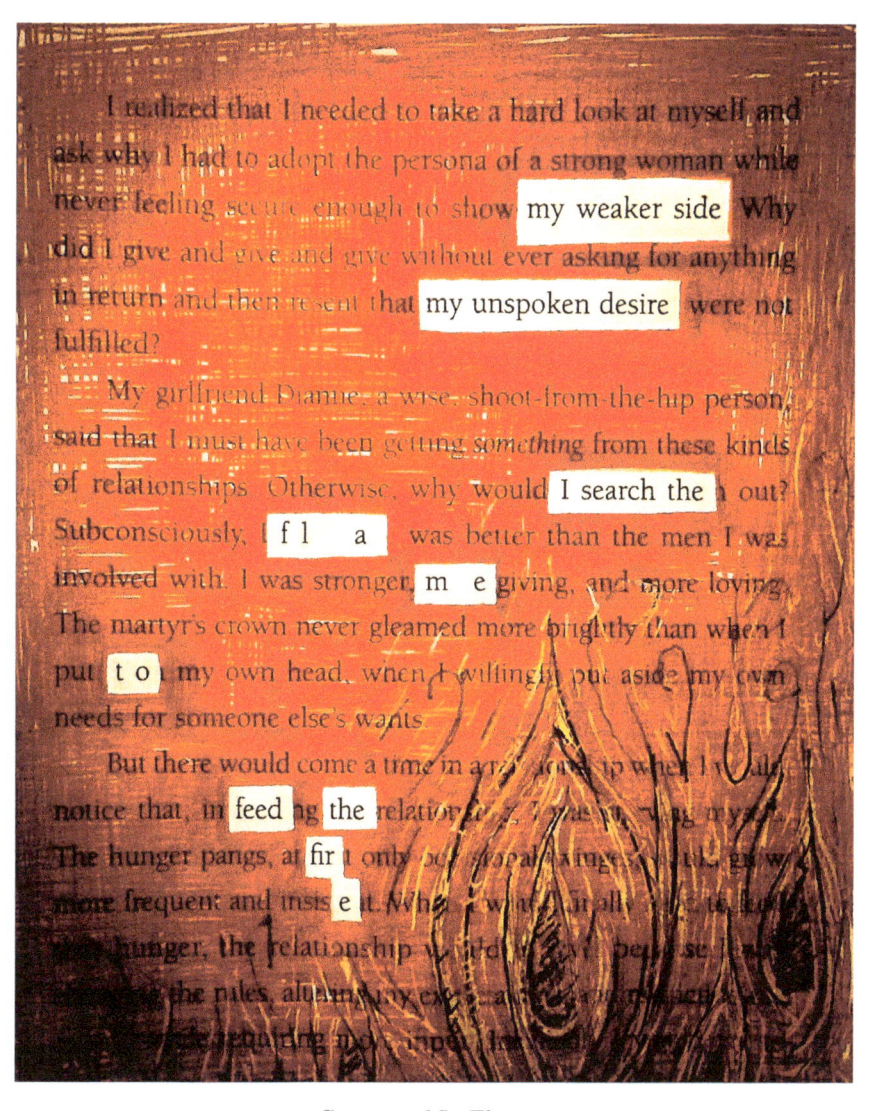

I realized that I needed to take a hard look at myself and ask why I had to adopt the persona of a strong woman while never feeling secure enough to show my weaker side. Why did I give and give and give without ever asking for anything in return and then resent that my unspoken desire were not fulfilled?

My girlfriend Dianne, a wise, shoot-from-the-hip person, said that I must have been getting *something* from these kinds of relationships. Otherwise, why would I search the out? Subconsciously, f l a was better than the men I was involved with. I was stronger, m e giving, and more loving. The martyr's crown never gleamed more brightly than when I put t o my own head, when I willingly put aside my own needs for someone else's wants.

But there would come a time in a when I notice that, in feed g the relation The hunger pangs, at fir t only more frequent and insis e t. Wh hunger, the relationship the rules, alt

Consumed In Flames

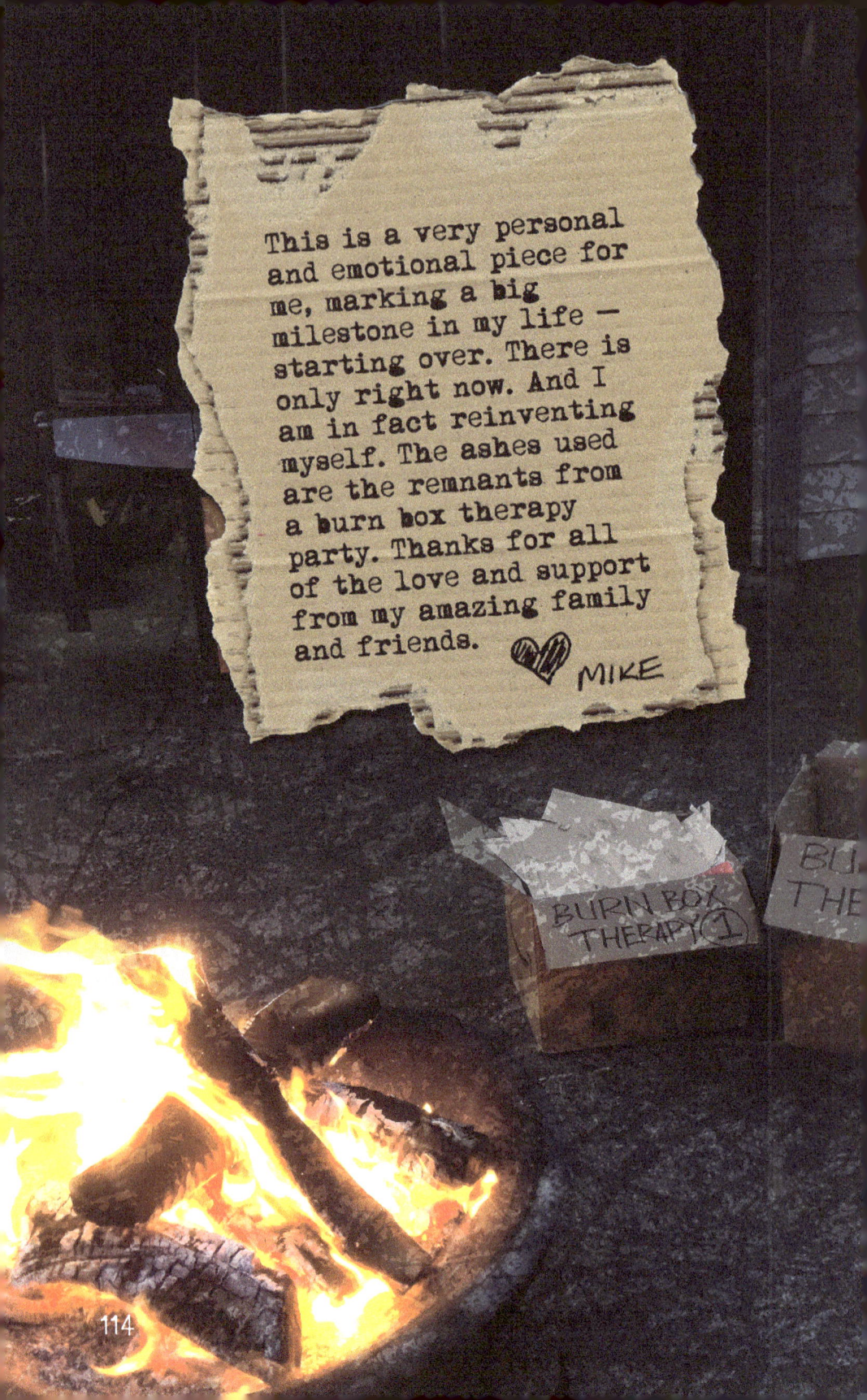

This is a very personal and emotional piece for me, marking a big milestone in my life — starting over. There is only right now. And I am in fact reinventing myself. The ashes used are the remnants from a burn box therapy party. Thanks for all of the love and support from my amazing family and friends.

MIKE

Rising From The Ashes

instruction manuals.

with

you

do
not

come

ghostly heart of mysteries undivulged in autumn.

Secrets Of The Fall

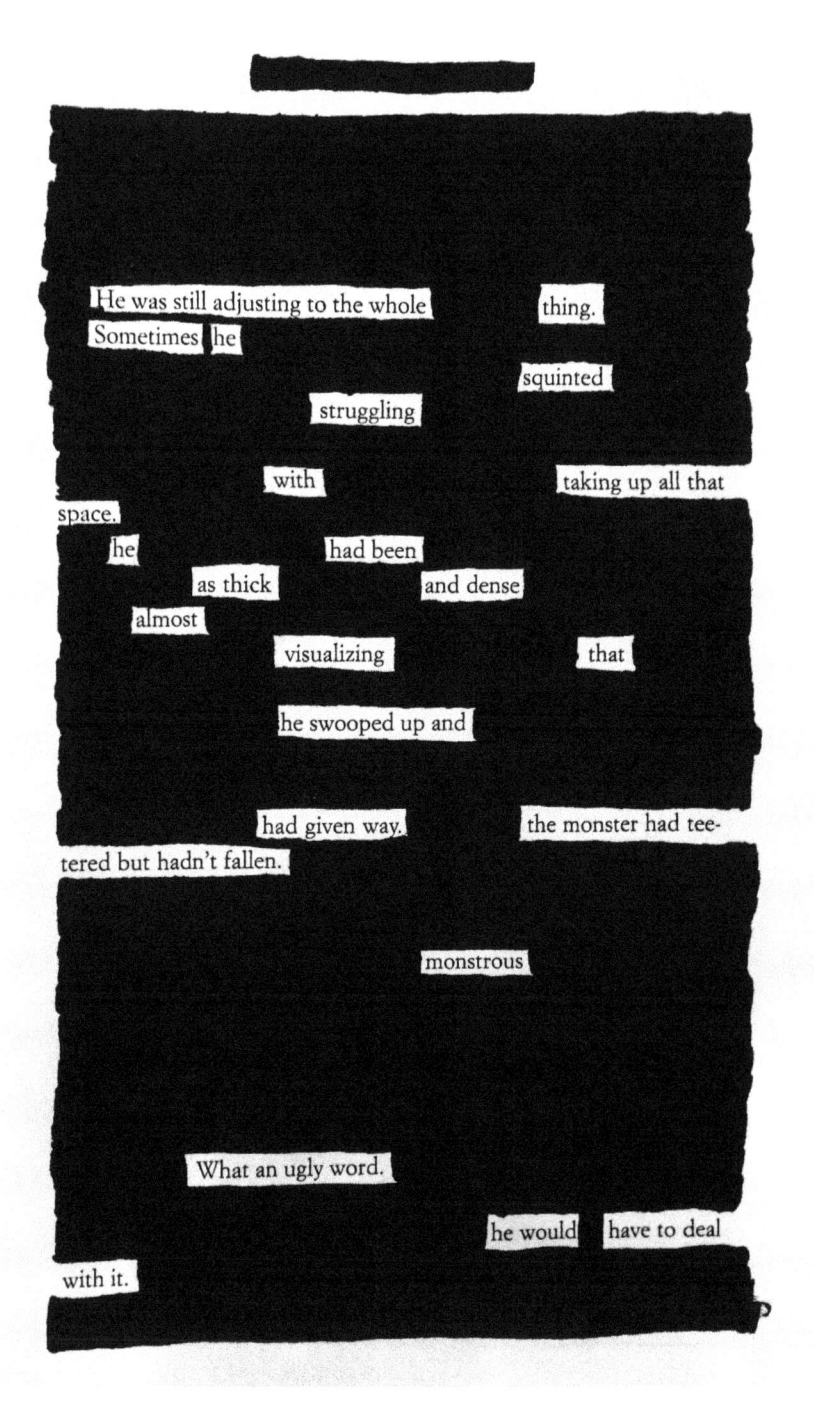

He was still adjusting to the whole thing. Sometimes he squinted struggling with taking up all that space. he had been as thick and dense almost visualizing that he swooped up and had given way. the monster had teetered but hadn't fallen.

monstrous

What an ugly word. he would have to deal with it.

Monstrous - My very first attempt at Blackout Poetry

hold on too tightly,

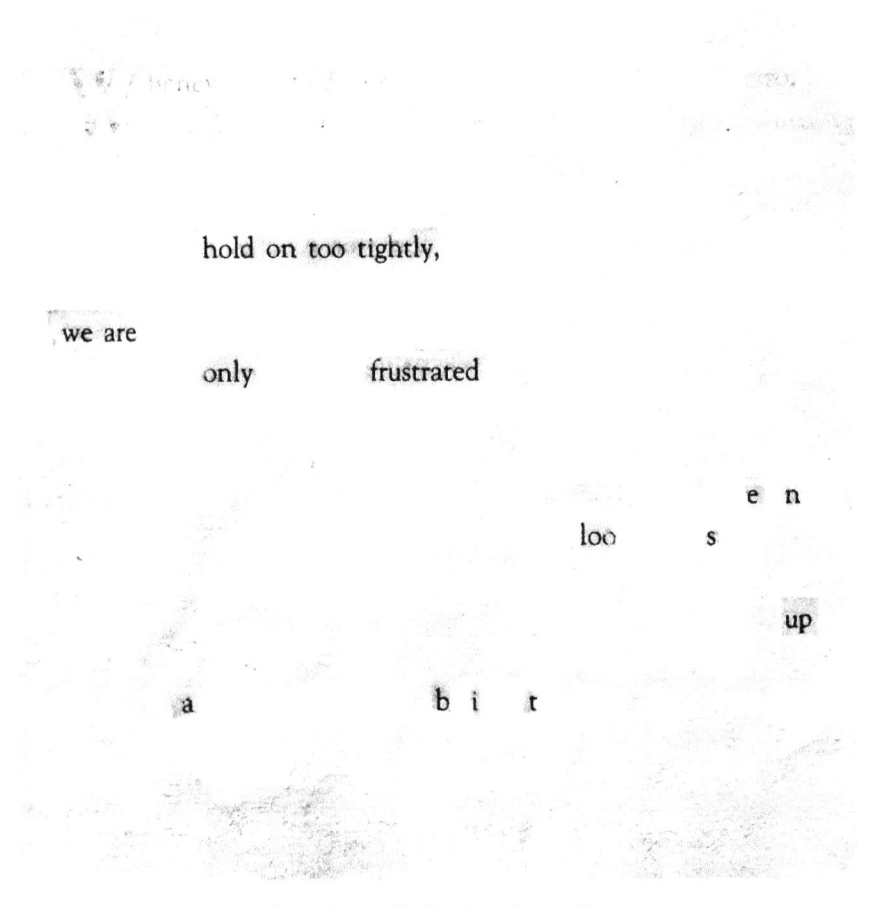

we are

only   frustrated

                    e n
              loo s

                         up

    a   b i t

Blackout Poem Haiku for #bpchallenges

once you
realize you have
wings
you can train
yourself
to fly

Learning To Fly

stay

I'll meet you there, love
Where the sky kisses the sea
And we can dwell in that place
Lost together
Somewhere on the horizon
Until the sun sinks into
The oceans deep inviting embrace
And the damp moon appears
to influence the tides
Pulled into a gravitational dance
As we sway rhythmically back and forth
In unison

And we can
Stay

together in that place
To watch the sun rise again
Splashing colorful morning kisses
Upon its one true love
Forever bound with certainty
An unconditional attraction
Where promises are kept
Somewhere on the horizon
Until you are the sky
And I am the sea

dwelling together, where the sky and sea, appear to meet:

On The Horizon

"They're taking a hell of a chance

"For

good reasons.

and

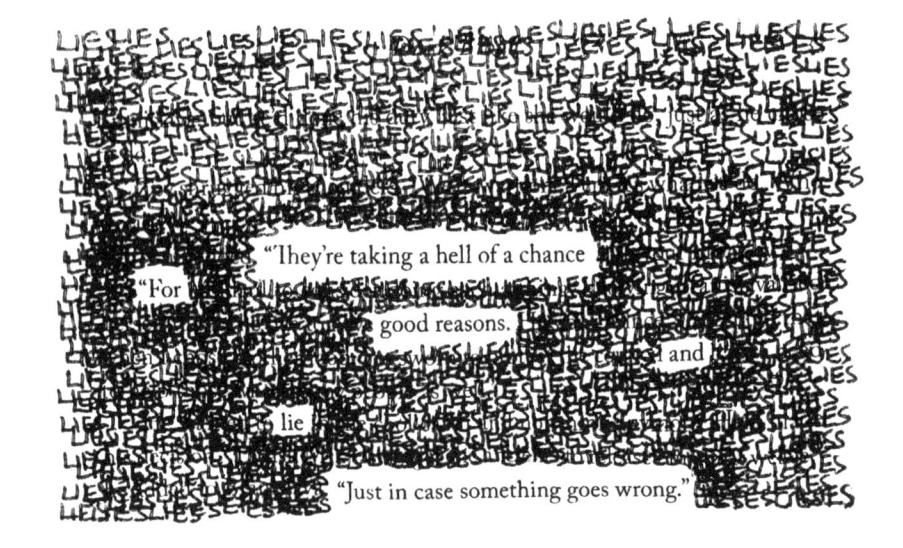

lie

"Just in case something goes wrong."

Surrounded By Lies

> slash-and-burn baby a blackout is gonna make us look even better.

Slash And Burn Blackout

I believe in you

In case you needed to hear it today...

If
not
now
when?

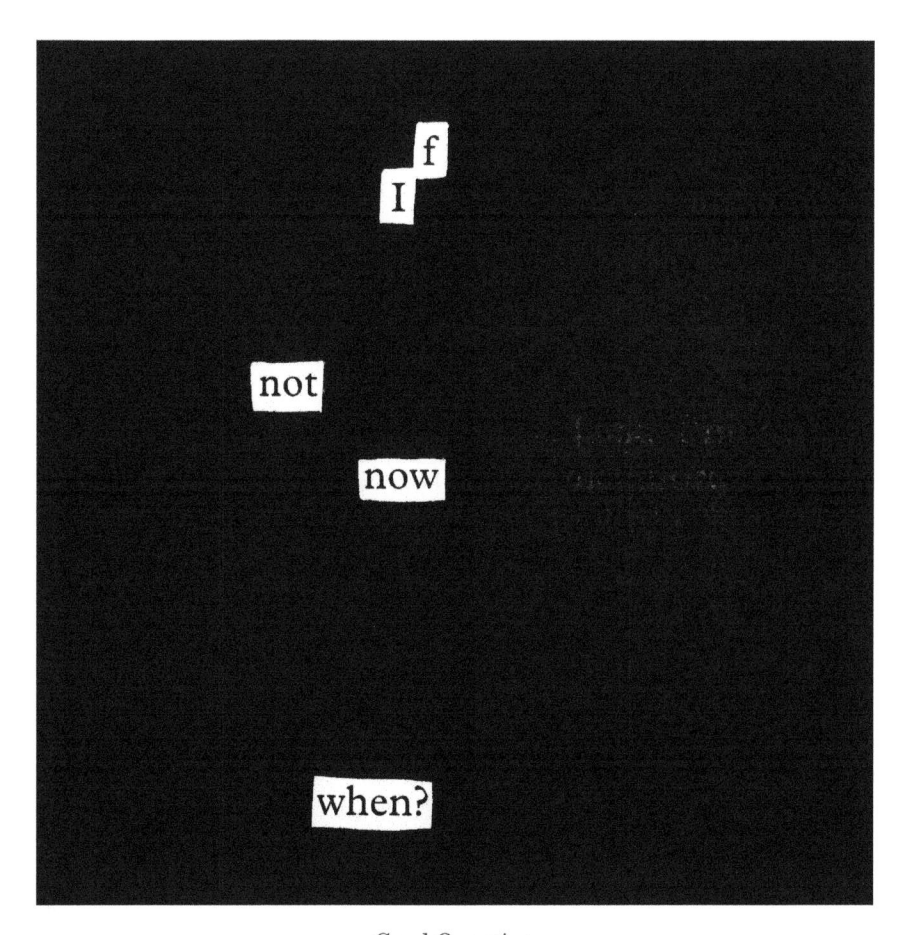

Good Question

an invisible thread connects those who are destined to meet, regardless of time, place, or circumstance. the thread may stretch or tangle, but it will never break.

— Ancient Chinese Proverb

> being of the same shape,
>
>
> between
> the inner and outer   is
>   of the greatest charms in the
>
>   tangle
>
>   of
>
>   l
>   ove

Perfect Fit

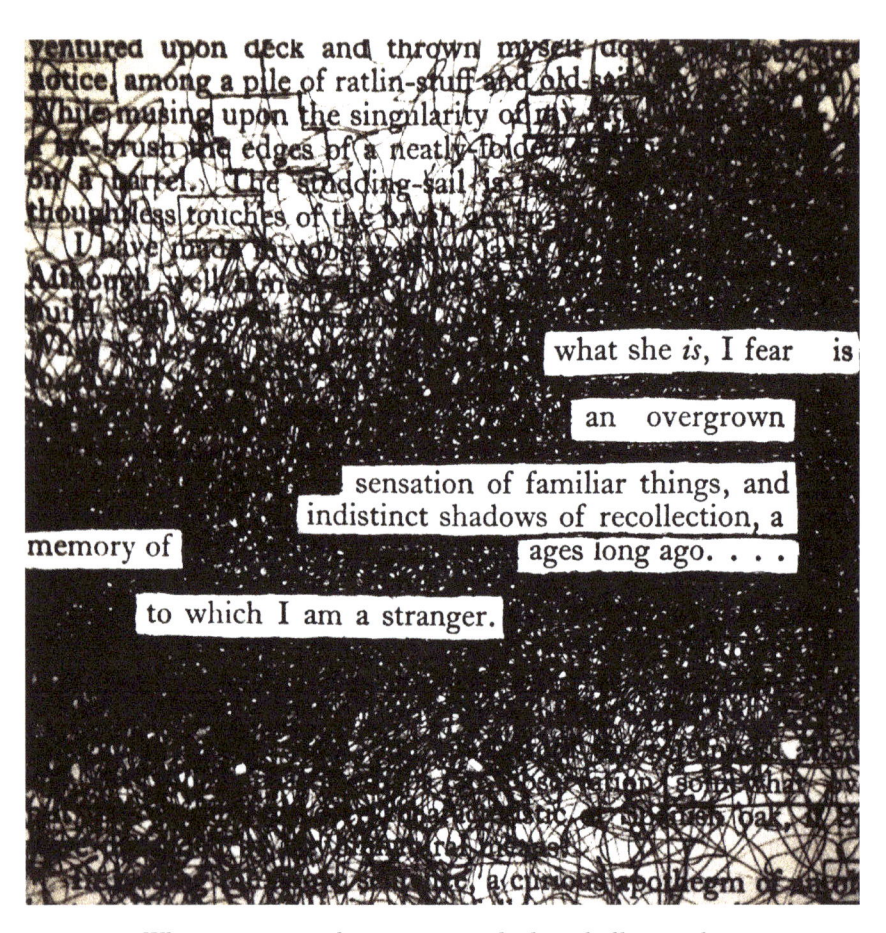

what she *is*, I fear is an overgrown sensation of familiar things, and indistinct shadows of recollection, a memory of ages long ago.... to which I am a stranger.

What you were, what you are and what shall never be...

This journey beyond sleep, seemed awkward

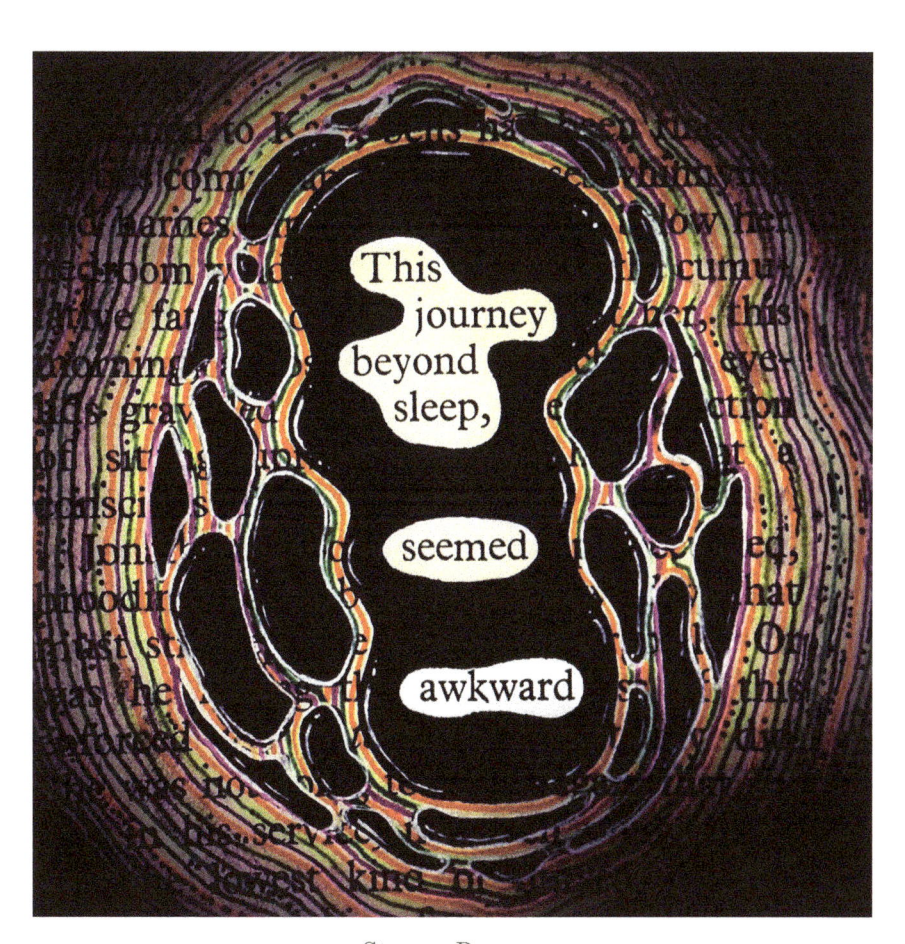

Strange Dreams

I'm (Barely Visible)

never

Doubt

yourself

Nothing Is Impossible

the secret that leads
to many goals
is tenacity.

– Fortune Cookie Saying

Tenacious

Love

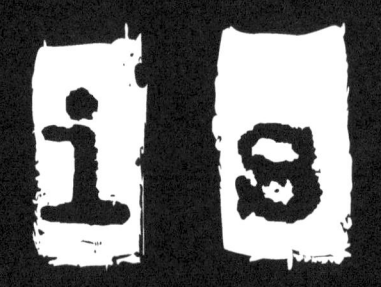

is

not perfect

> remember the sound of laughter snow coated

Seasonal Impression

do

all right on your own

Self Dependence

don't worry about a thing

'Cause every little thing gonna be alright - A Tribute To Bob Marley

we all

have

moments of

weakness

Kryptonite

we all want to be
loved and proclaim our
love. whether its our
significant other,
family, friends or even
a simple kind gesture
towards someone we
dont know...love is truly
the best gift we could
ever give or receive.
love is all we have when
there is nothing
else left.

Love makes each other's imperfections **beaut if ul**

Perfectly Imperfect

y ou
my
home

You

ling er

everywhere.

It's like magic

Home Is Where The Heart Is

She sat for a few moments

as
the
Tears

streamed down her face.
She would never see him again.

November Rain

whispered

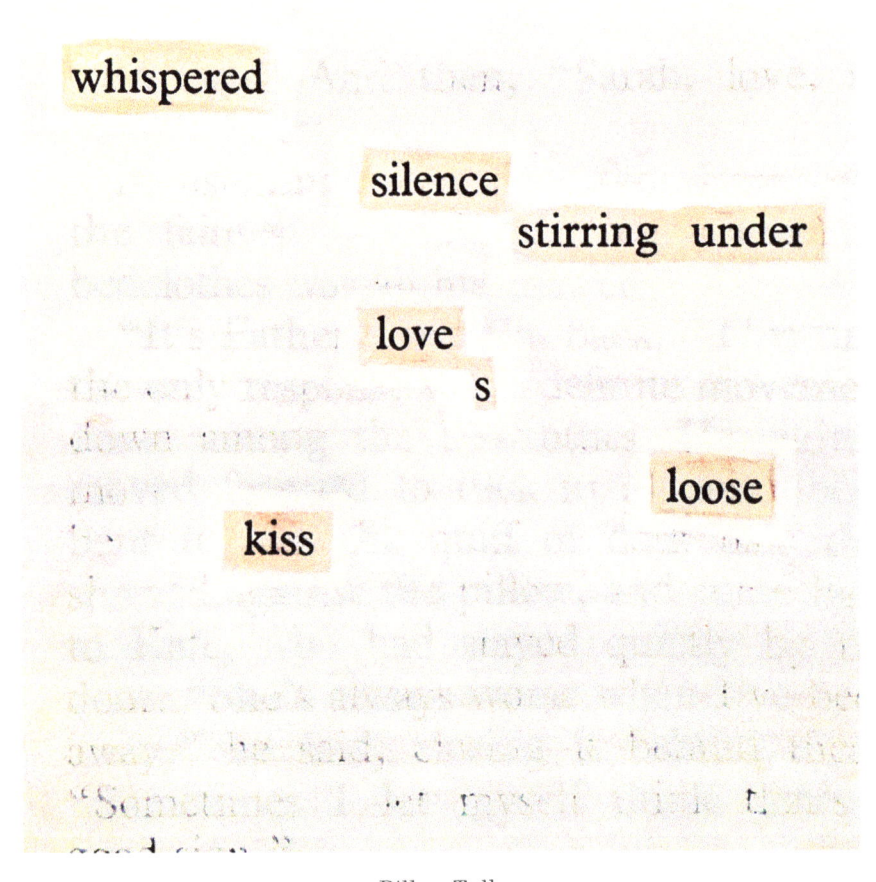

        silence

                stirring under

       love
          s

                    loose

    kiss

Pillow Talk

follow

the

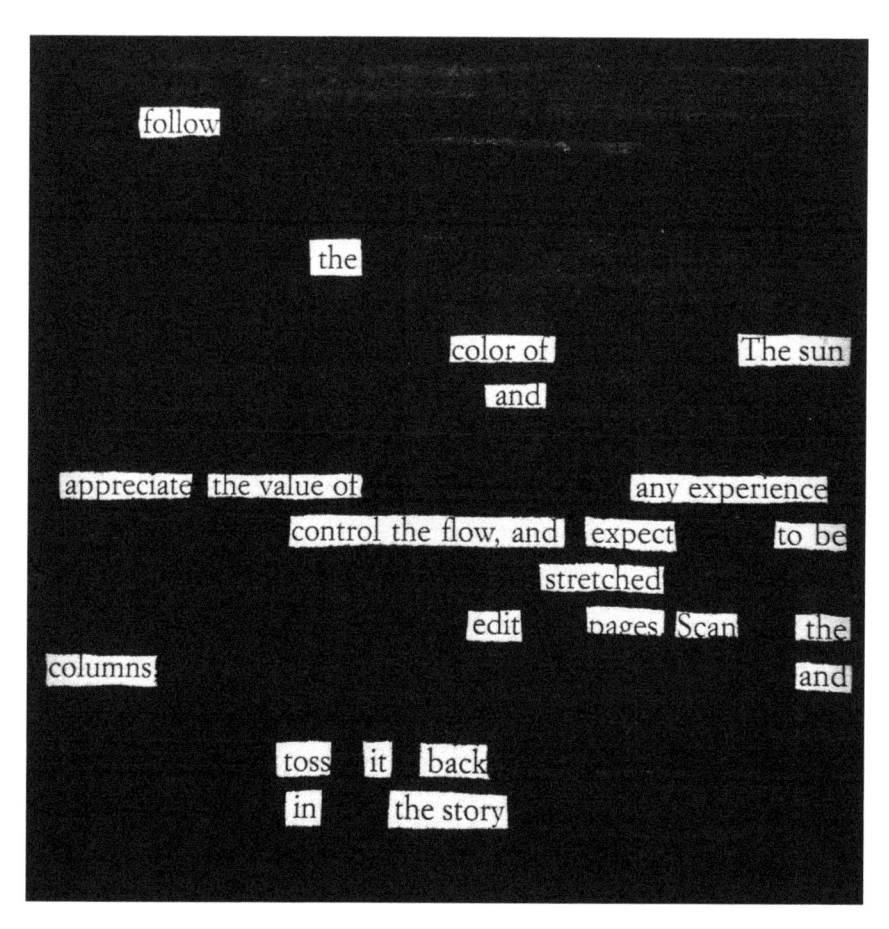

color of　　　　　　　The sun
and

appreciate the value of　　　any experience
control the flow, and expect   to be
stretched
edit   pages Scan   the
columns   and

toss it back
in the story

Novel Approach

If not for love what holds thy grace?
A lonely moon in a night time sky.
An unfelt touch.
An empty vase.
To still the air and calm the tides.

If not for love what comfort holds
to dry the tears of a stronghold heart.
A hundred days of a thousand nights.
Both join as one then
slowly part.

his thoughts.
Under the Stars?"
Being with her again
never forget she
light
his was

11:11

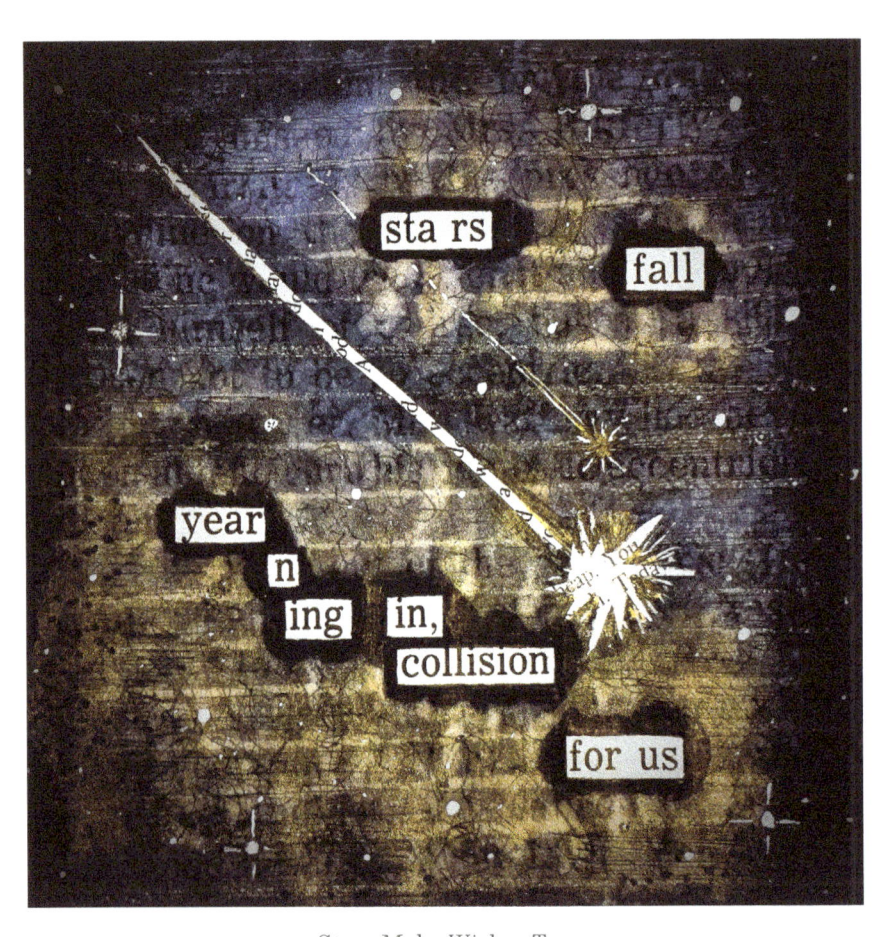

Stars Make Wishes Too

his chest

overwhelmed
                    felt

    weather patterns

                    almost like pain
he walked
                in
                    her
    direction.
        as though she was

    the rain

Chance Of Precipitation

some idiot in an ape costume

entered the

ZOO

Monkey Business

> I wanted to see
>
> cloudiness felt
>
> More important
>
> traces but I

In A Fog

Our souls entwined
In some strange magnetic attraction
Both of us yearning
Needing to be
It was always a question of when
Forever answered with one simple word
Like a song left on repeat
(Soon)
From off in the distance
The faint sound of rumbling thunder
Like little white lies
Seemingly harmless
Growing louder and clearer
More aware of it's imminent arrival
(Soon)
A sudden outburst of veracious words
Raining with disbelief
Left us soaking in reticence
As the wild white storm rolled in
Ravenous and greedy
Tearing the words from our mouths
Devouring the flesh from our very bones
The savage beast
Settled down to rest
Digesting what was left
Of our whole existence and half-truths
Until there was nothing left
But silence
And we

Were

N o

M

o

r

e

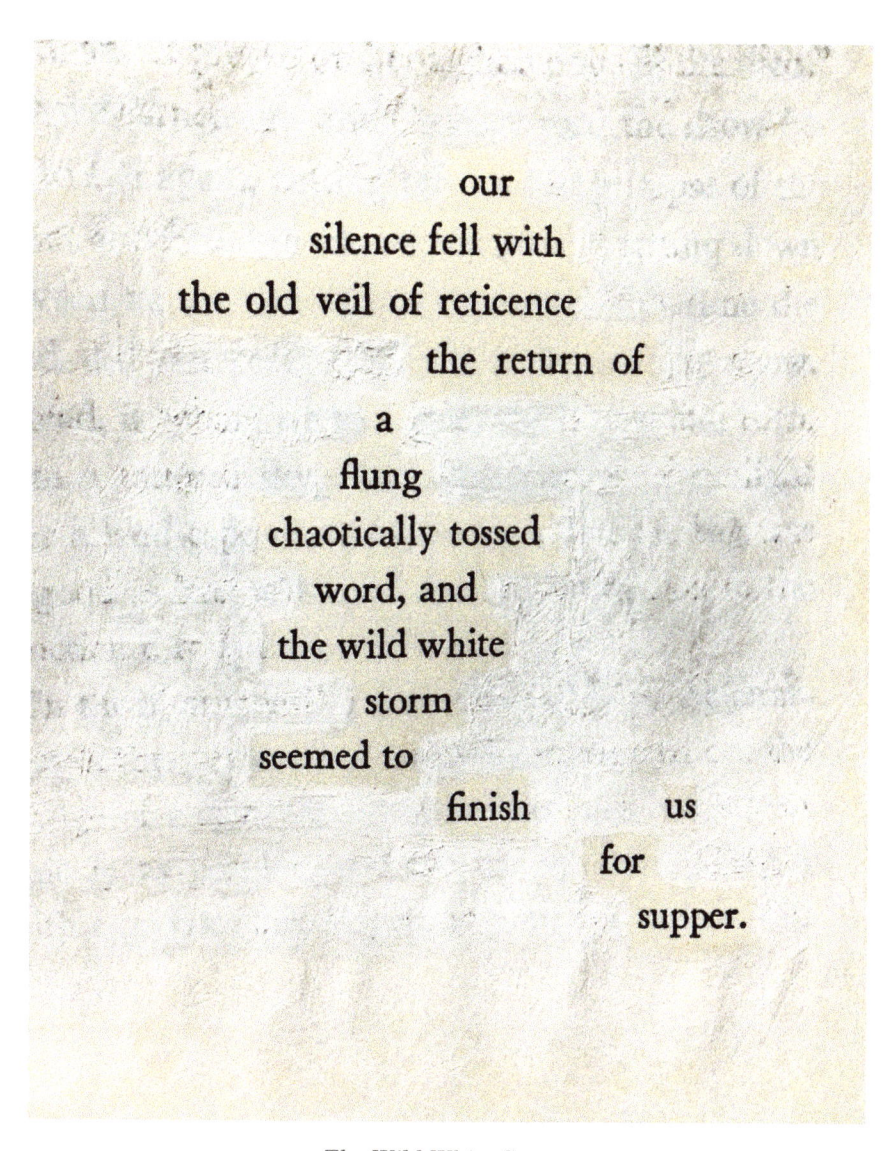

         our
   silence fell with
the old veil of reticence
               the return of
           a
         flung
   chaotically tossed
       word, and
    the wild white
         storm
      seemed to
              finish   us
                         for
                            supper.

The Wild White Storm

magic

out there,

believing

is

secret

is

the

passion

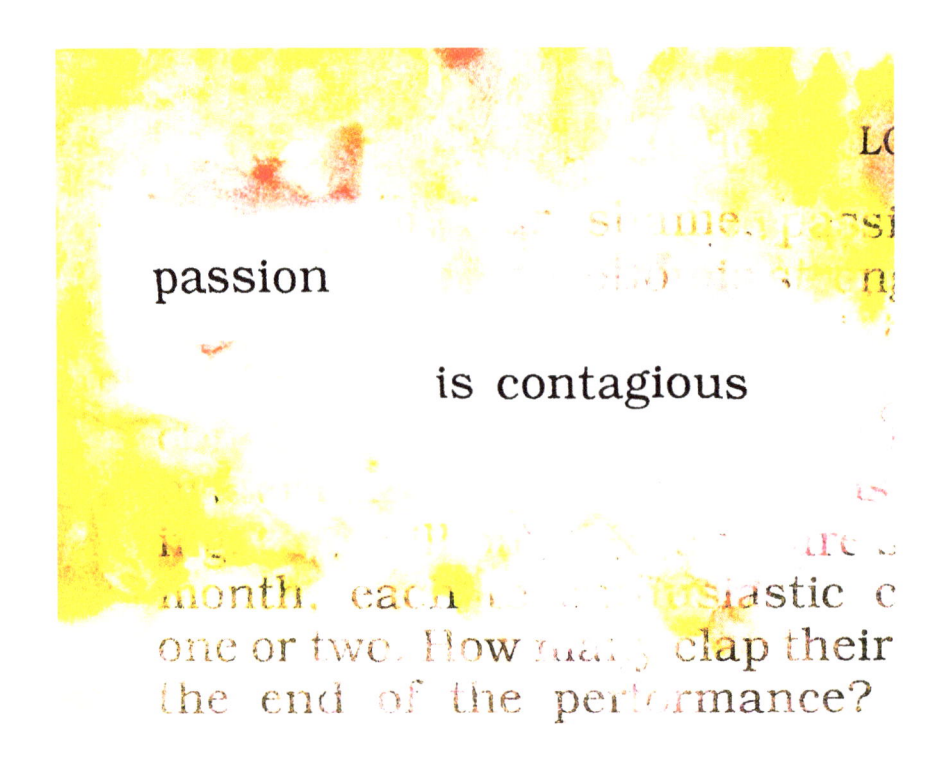

is contagious

Find your passion. Share it. Watch it spread.

I burrow through
my real-world garden,
and
There are emotions deeply rooted that
grow like weeds.
if

I
relive the pain, but I keep digging
a little
buried
sunshine
of my inner
thoughts
as any gardener will tell you,
is only the beginning
and the enjoyment
of weeding

Weed And Feed For The Soul

Keep Your Eyes On The Road (Detail)

you
can   only
move forward
the past
is
in the rearview mirror

Keep Your Eyes On The Road

you are worth more than you think.

change is what is needed to perpetuate ourselves.

Self Worth

This

day

represents freedom

Friends and family

Independence Day

blank

...that's all I feel

my soul is

stretched

With

d e   pression
and
dressed in a stranger's ill-fitting

silence

Well Worn

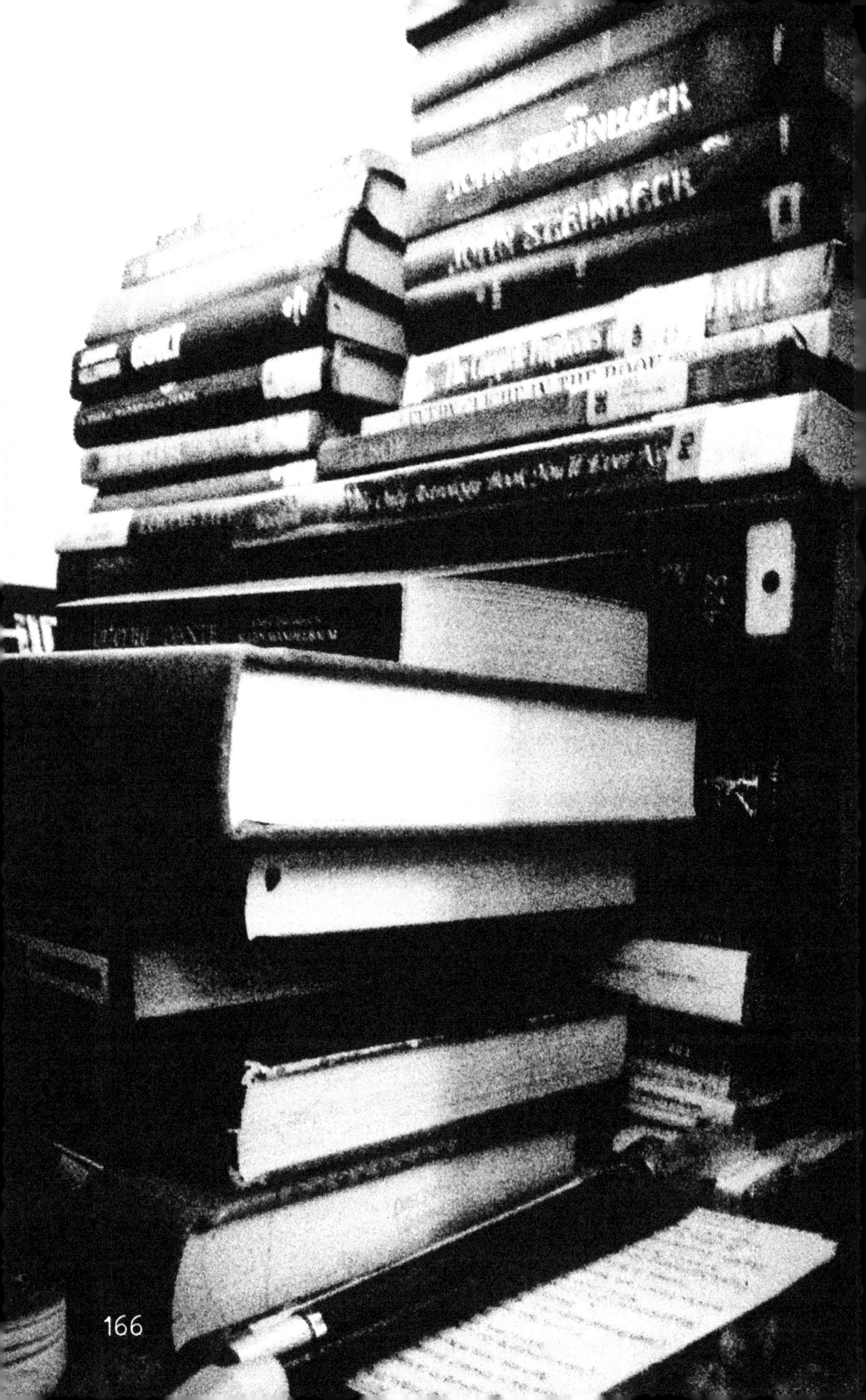

STEINBECK
STEINBECK

promises become friends: to help and make refresh the soul, ourselves a happier group of people

For Bee

spread continually joy everywhere

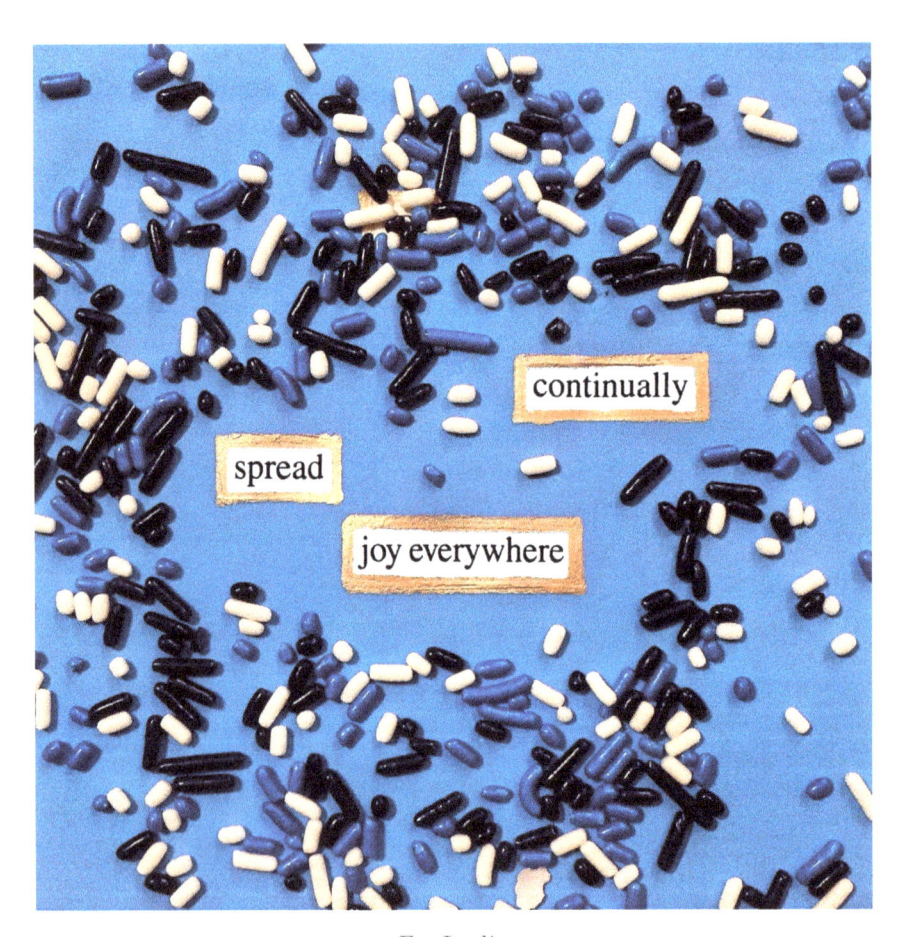

For Leslie

It came from above, somewhere in the tree.

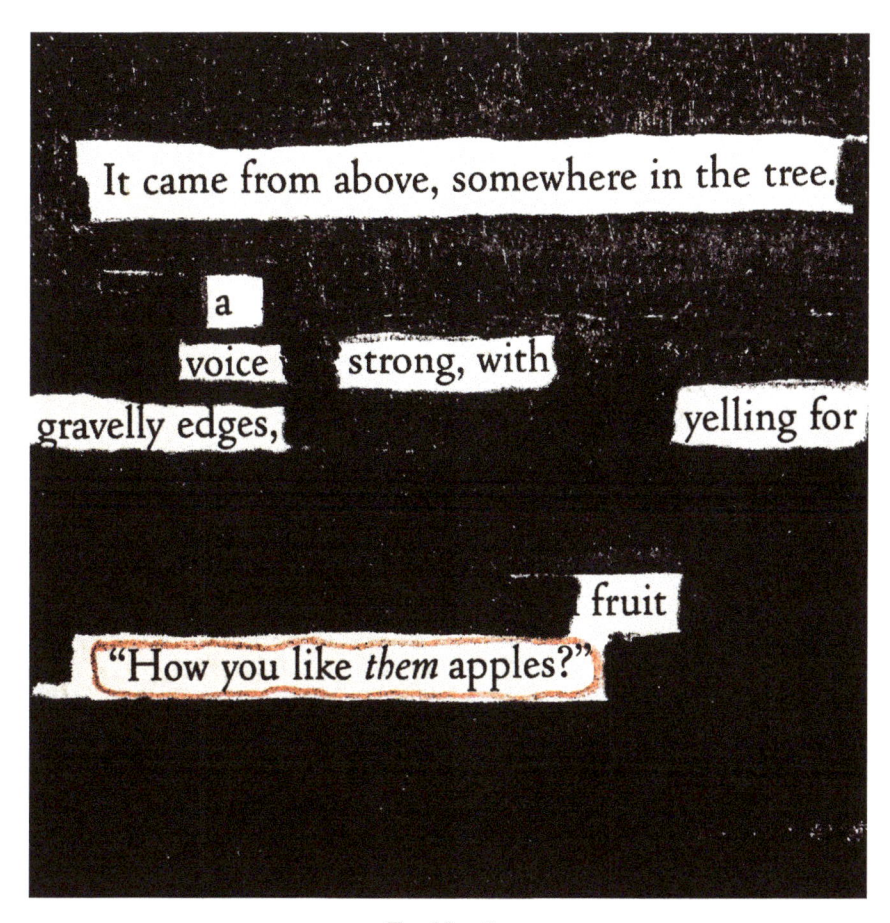

a voice   strong, with
gravelly edges,   yelling for

fruit
"How you like *them* apples?"

For Martin

She stared at that wispy mustache of love

For Brenda (Mama Blackout)

love is

worth the risk.

For John (The Godfather of Blackout Poetry)

What is your

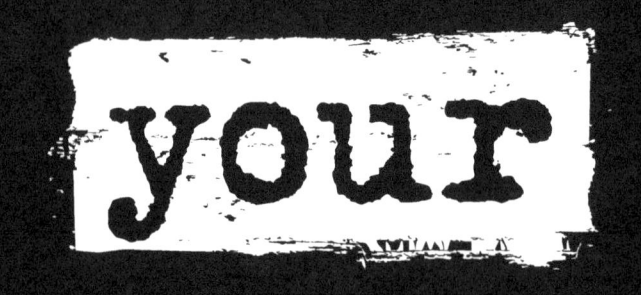

Why?

THIS IS NOT
THE END

about the author

Michael Nyers is a designer, mixed media artist, ENFJ, mental health advocate, doer, dreamer, and all around funny guy from Youngstown, Ohio. Mike's passion is blackout poetry, which he sees as a look into the subconscious mind that can promote mindfulness and creativity, benefiting overall well-being and mental health.

www.fadeintoablackoutpoetry.com
www.instagram.com/fade.into.a.blackout
www.instagram.com/blackoutpoetrychallenges
www.facebook.com/fadeintoablackout
#fadeintoablackout

BLACKOUT POETRY

Fade into a Blackout

ART + WORDS + WELLNESS

CPSIA information can be obtained
at www.ICGtesting.com
Printed in the USA
BVHW09s0608140818
524433BV00006B/6/P

9 780936 014241